DECLINE AND DECAY

STRATEGIES FOR SURVIVING THE COMING UNPLEASANTNESS

A. AMERICAN AND ALAN KAY

NOTICE TO THE READER:

We would like to take a moment to make a few things crystal clear about the authors. The only use of violence we recognize as lawful and acceptable is for self-defense. No one can denounce the use of violence to defend the defenseless from the merciless. Our children, our elderly, our families, homes, community and nation are all worthy of defense. Up to and including our very lives.

We do not advocate the overthrow or usurpation of lawful, legal authority. We are not militia members, even though our Constitution recognizes militias: We have friends from all strata of society. In our eyes, we are all Americans, first. <u>WE FIRMLY BELIEVE IN INDIVIDUAL LIBERTY.</u>

We will support the rights of those we disagree with, for if their rights are not safe, neither are ours, or yours for that matter. This book is not written for any particular segment of society, it is for all Americans, for that moment when no one is coming to save you.

With these thoughts in mind, and the fact we live in a litigious society, here's the legal stuff. We are not lawyers! (But we have known a few and didn't really care for them.) The information in this book is intended to make you think. To evaluate your personal state of readiness to deal with the unforeseen. It is incumbent on you, dear reader, to check all local, state and Federal laws, regulations, edicts, proclamations, you get the idea, before taking any action.

The information provided herein is intended to encourage self-reliance. It is not a blueprint of exactly what to do. You must consider your personal situation and adapt the ideas shared to meet your needs.

In so doing, it is the author's sincere hope you will develop a community focused on self-reliance. Become proactive, not reactive.

While we whole heartedly encourage the ownership and lawful use and carry of firearms, do not enter into this skill set without first learning emergency trauma care. There are precious few second chances when firearms are involved.

The contents you are about to read are for *informational* purposes only. Any actions you undertake are your own and you will be held legally accountable for them.

In memory of Harold "The Otter" Weatherman. Old Dude knew the world was changing and we talked about it often. Your time was cut short but you damn sure made the most of it. I'm not putting dates of his life here; to me, he's not gone. He' still here and I talk to him every day. Miss you, Old Dude.

Alan, I owe you a debt of gratitude I can never repay. The fact you were there that long day and night that Dad finally said enough is enough, meant more to me and mom than words can describe. We had a good time over those hours, filled with laughter and smiles. It was a good death and for that, I thank you.

Table of Contents

In these uncertain times we are living in, it's worth taking a minute to look back at the early days of this once great nation. With that said, take a minute to read this and seriously consider it.

Patrick Henry, St. John's Church, Richmond, Virginia
March 23, 1775[1].

MR. PRESIDENT: No man thinks more highly than I do of the patriotism, as well as abilities, of the very worthy gentlemen who have just addressed the House. But different men often see the same subject in different lights; and, therefore, I hope it will not be thought disrespectful to those gentlemen if, entertaining as I do, opinions of a character very opposite to theirs, I shall speak forth my sentiments freely, and without reserve. This is no time for ceremony. The question before the House is one of awful moment to this country. For my own part, I consider it as nothing less than a question of freedom or slavery; and in proportion to the magnitude of the subject ought to be the freedom of the debate. It is only in this way that we can hope to arrive at truth, and fulfil the great responsibility which we hold to God and our country. Should I keep back my opinions at such a time, through fear of giving offence, I should consider myself as guilty of treason towards my country, and of an act of disloyalty toward the majesty of heaven, which I revere above all earthly kings.

1   *Source:* Wirt, William. *Sketches of the Life and Character of Patrick Henry* (Philadelphia) 1836, as reproduced in *The World's Great Speeches*, Lewis Copeland and Lawrence W. Lamm, eds., (New York) 1973.

Mr. President, it is natural to man to indulge in the illusions of hope. We are apt to shut our eyes against a painful truth, and listen to the song of that siren till she transforms us into beasts. Is this the part of wise men, engaged in a great and arduous struggle for liberty? Are we disposed to be of the number of those who, having eyes, see not, and, having ears, hear not, the things which so nearly concern their temporal salvation? For my part, whatever anguish of spirit it may cost, I am willing to know the whole truth; to know the worst, and to provide for it.

I have but one lamp by which my feet are guided; and that is the lamp of experience. I know of no way of judging of the future but by the past. And judging by the past, I wish to know what there has been in the conduct of the British ministry for the last ten years, to justify those hopes with which gentlemen have been pleased to solace themselves, and the House? Is it that insidious smile with which our petition has been lately received? Trust it not, sir; it will prove a snare to your feet. Suffer not yourselves to be betrayed with a kiss. Ask yourselves how this gracious reception of our petition comports with these war-like preparations which cover our waters and darken our land. Are fleets and armies necessary to a work of love and reconciliation? Have we shown ourselves so unwilling to be reconciled, that force must be called in to win back our love? Let us not deceive ourselves, sir. These are the implements of war and subjugation; the last arguments to which kings resort. I ask, gentlemen, sir, what means this martial array, if its purpose be not to force us to submission? Can gentlemen assign any other possible motive for it? Has Great Britain any enemy, in this quarter of the world, to call for all this accumulation of navies and armies? No, sir, she has none. They are meant for us; they can be meant for no other. They are sent over to bind and rivet upon us those chains which the British ministry have been so long forging. And what have we to oppose to them? Shall we try argument? Sir, we have been trying that for the last ten years. Have we anything new to offer upon the subject? Nothing. We have held the subject up in every light of which it is capable; but it has been all in vain. Shall we resort to entreaty and humble supplication? What terms shall we find which have not been already exhausted? Let us not, I beseech you, sir, deceive ourselves. Sir, we have done everything that could be done, to avert the storm which is now coming on. We have petitioned; we have remonstrated; we have supplicated; we have prostrated ourselves before the throne and have implored its interposition to arrest the tyrannical hands of the ministry and Parliament. Our petitions have been slighted; our remonstrances have produced additional violence and insult; our supplications have been disregarded; and we have been spurned, with contempt, from the foot of the throne. In vain, after these things, may we indulge the fond hope of peace and reconciliation. There is no longer any room for hope. If we wish to be free, if we mean to preserve inviolate those inestimable privileges for which we have been so long contending, if we mean not basely to abandon the noble struggle in which we have been so long engaged, and which we have pledged ourselves never to abandon until the glorious object of our contest shall be obtained, we must fight! I repeat it, sir, we must fight! An appeal to arms and to the God of Hosts is all that is left us!

They tell us, sir, that we are weak; unable to cope with so formidable an adversary. But when shall we be stronger? Will it be the next week, or the next year? Will it be when we are totally disarmed, and when a British guard shall be stationed in every house? Shall we gather strength by irresolution and inaction? Shall we acquire the means of effectual resistance, by lying supinely on our backs, and hugging the delusive phantom of hope, until our enemies shall have bound us hand and foot? Sir, we are not weak if we make a proper use of those means which the God of nature hath placed in our power. Three millions of people, armed in the holy cause of liberty, and in such a country as that which we possess, are invincible by any force which our enemy can send against us. Besides, sir, we shall not fight our battles alone. There is a just God who presides over the destinies of nations; and who will raise up friends to fight our battles for us. The battle, sir, is not to the strong alone; it is to the vigilant, the active, the brave. Besides, sir, we have no election. If we were base enough to desire it, it is now too late to retire from the contest. There is no retreat but in submission and slavery! Our chains are forged! Their clanking may be heard on the plains of Boston! The war is inevitable and let it come! I repeat it, sir, let it come.

It is in vain, sir, to extenuate the matter. Gentlemen may cry, Peace, Peace, but there is no peace. The war is actually begun! The next gale that sweeps from the north will bring to our ears the clash of resounding arms! Our brethren are already in the field! Why stand we here idle? What is it that gentlemen wish? What would they have? Is life so dear, or peace so sweet, as to be purchased at the price of chains and slavery? Forbid it, Almighty God! I know not what course others may take; but as for me, give me liberty or give me death!

Foreword

For perspective, this book was started two years ago. Due to the requirements of life and schedules, we had to work when we could get together, as this book could not have happened any other way. It took the two of us, sitting side by side, to complete it. Then COVID came and travel was restricted, a delay no one could have foreseen. When travel was once again allowed, we were stymied yet again by civil unrest and the uncertainties that brought with it. All the while, we felt the urgency growing to complete the project.

And as these words are being typed there is talk of yet another lockdown. Recent events made many of the statements contained here appear prescient, to us, as we know where the country was when we began. We cannot see into the future; we possess no crystal ball. However, we are students of history and careful observers of the times we live in. Most of these predictions were obvious to anyone paying attention. And while we know not what the future holds in store for our nation, for us as a people, we feel confident in saying, more troubling times lie ahead.

The 2020 election looms on the horizon and a cloud of uncertainty is building around it. Heed the ideas and concepts laid out in the following, time is running out. Welcome to The Quickening.

The game is coming, and you are going to play it!

A note to you, the reader. Nothing between these covers is a substitute for training. Everything contained here is the opinions of the authors. In no way do we claim for any of the content to be the only way or even the best way. Each is simply a way. Your mileage may vary.

Survival situations are not limited to the wilderness. The end of the world *as you know it*, can arrive at home, on your way to work, at school or in the grocery store. We are now at a place we have never been before in society. Our world is rapidly changing, as are the threats we must face. With those thoughts in mind, we must step back and rethink the term survival. The game is coming, and you WILL play the game. No one will be on the sidelines; it will not be a spectator sport. Participation will be compulsory. You will adapt to this new reality and learn to survive; or you will not.

Introduction

HUMANS HAVE EXISTED ON THIS planet for quite some time using nothing more than the natural materials found around them. An elder teacher once said, *everything you need is within twenty feet of you at any time*. Our ancestors not only survived, they thrived.

Regardless of our technological advances, little has changed, except for the fact that we now live in a glass castle. The frailty of our current society is at unprecedented levels. Just-In-Time inventory and the removal of the masses from the source of their food has created an incredibly complex system that is simply unsustainable.

Evolutionarily speaking, we are not far removed from our hunter-gatherer forbearers. However, the skills and instinct that enabled our thriving has atrophied and nearly vanished. The modern human is now so far removed from his natural habitat that most simply cannot survive in the very environment to which they are biologically engineered. Most modern humans can now only survive in a wholly artificial environment of their own creation. The average person dropped into the wild and left to their own devices would soon perish.

The nature of humans hasn't really changed. We still compete for resources and slaughter one another wholesale. Only now, that competition is taken to a higher level; and as we can all see on the nightly news, the slaughter occurs on an industrial scale.

Nature is cruel and unforgiving. At this very moment, physically near you, something is killing something else to survive. If left unguarded, the young and defenseless are plucked from the nest and mercilessly consumed. The snake catches the rat and consumes him with no thought of the rat's life. He then stretches out on a rock to warm himself and digest his full belly. Then the hawk swoops in and snatches up the snake with no thought of the snake or knowledge of the rat. If left unguarded, your family and your possessions will be preyed upon.

We are currently witnessing a de-evolutionary spiral, a social decline. The frailty of our current system is alarming; there is little margin for error. Our current patterns of life are wholly unsustainable. One need only look through the window of history for a glimpse of the horrors of which man is capable. A great deal of time could be spent discussing potential threats. In fact, such a topic could be a book in itself. Such thinking is largely wasted energy and leads to mental paralysis.

It really doesn't matter if we are subjected to an economic collapse, an electromagnetic pulse or yet another war in the endless line of wars. What's coming will come and it's beyond the scope of our power as individuals to prevent it. Your requirements to sustain life will be the same regardless of the life changing event.

You must satisfy these needs in order to survive

- Water
- Shelter
- Fire (Energy)
- Food
- Medicine
- Security
- Sanitation
- *Community* (The lone wolf is a dead wolf)

We as individuals cannot influence the course of world events. It seems, we can't even rein in our own corrupt government. We must focus on the things that *are* within our power. We must control the controllable. We can't cause Congress to balance the checkbook and embrace sound economic policy. However, as an individual, I can push away from the table and embrace practices that make me healthier. I can, and do, regularly put on a heavy rucksack and go for a run. I can do exercises that make me stronger and thus harder to kill.

I can embrace the fact that the only consistent thing in life is the inconsistency. Every day of life is school; and we never graduate. The ability to adapt rapidly to changing events is a real asset. No one is coming to save you! You are your own first responder.

When the fecal matter hits the oscillator and energetically disassembles at high velocity, prep time is over. The time to realize you should always carry a tourniquet and master its use IS NOT as the dust clears from your car wreck and you notice your child is bleeding out! Your personal Armageddon may be coming sooner than you think. Be ready. If someone attacks you, having already decided to revoke your birth certificate, it would behoove you to kill them first. There is no such thing as second place or a participation trophy in the struggle of life and death.

1 - The Mental Stuff

"All things are ready, if our mind be so."
—William Shakespeare

YOUR MIND IS THE GREATEST survival tool of all. In my opinion, survival is approximately 80% mental. At any given moment, we can find ourselves in throbbing ecstasy or utter intolerable hell. It's really just a matter of our perspective and how we choose to embrace the challenges we face. My friend Dave Connell once said to me, "We are survival machines!" That we are. However, people are complex. We are at once spiritual, emotional, mental, physical and sexual creatures. What feats we are capable of!

Normalcy Bias

Normalcy bias is a dangerous phenomenon that we all must be careful of falling into. Wikipedia defines it this way:

> The *normalcy bias*, or *normality bias*, is a belief people hold when considering the possibility of a disaster. It causes people to underestimate both the likelihood of a disaster and its possible effects, because people believe that things will always function the way things normally have functioned. This may result in situations where people fail to adequately prepare themselves

1

for disasters, and on a larger scale, the failure of governments to include the populace in its disaster preparations. About 70% of people reportedly display normalcy bias in disasters.

The normalcy bias can manifest itself in various disasters, ranging from car crashes to world-historical events. It is hypothesized that the normalcy bias may be caused by the way the brain processes new information. Stress slows information processing, and when the brain cannot find an acceptable response to a situation, it fixates on a single and sometimes default solution. This single resolution can result in unnecessary injury or death in disaster situations. The lack of preparation for disasters often leads to inadequate shelter, supplies, and evacuation plans. Thus, normalcy bias can cause people to drastically underestimate the effects of the disaster and assume that everything will be all right. The negative effects of normalcy bias can be combatted through the four stages of disaster response: preparation, warning, impact, and aftermath. Normalcy bias has also been called *analysis paralysis*, *the ostrich effect*, and by first responders, *the negative panic*. The opposite of normalcy bias is overreaction, or worst-case scenario bias, in which small deviations from normality are dealt with as signals of an impending catastrophe.

Confirmation Bias

Just as with normalcy bias, we should carefully ensure that we are looking at things objectively, coming to our conclusion through reason and not emotion.

Wikipedia defines confirmation bias as follows:

Confirmation bias is the tendency to search for, interpret, favor, and recall information in a way that confirms one's preexisting beliefs or hypotheses. It is a type of cognitive bias and a systematic error of inductive reasoning. People display this bias when they gather or remember information selectively, or when they interpret it in a biased way. The effect is stronger for desired outcomes, emotionally charged issues, and for deeply entrenched beliefs.

People also tend to interpret ambiguous evidence as supporting their existing position. Biased search, interpretation and memory have been invoked to explain attitude polarization (when a disagreement becomes more extreme even though the different parties are exposed to the same evidence), belief perseverance (when beliefs persist after the evidence for them is shown to be false), the irrational primacy effect (a greater reliance on information encountered early in a series) and Illusory correlation (when people falsely perceive an association between two events or situations).

A series of psychological experiments in the 1960s suggested that people are biased toward confirming their existing beliefs. Later work re-interpreted these results as a tendency to test ideas in a one-sided way, focusing on one possibility and ignoring alternatives. In certain situations, this tendency can bias people's conclusions. Explanations for the observed biases include wishful thinking and the limited human capacity to process information. *Another explanation is that people show confirmation bias because they are weighing up the costs of being wrong, rather than investigating in a neutral, scientific way. However, even scientists and intelligent people can be prone to confirmation bias.* (Emphasis added by the authors)

Confirmation biases contribute to overconfidence in personal beliefs and can maintain or strengthen beliefs in the face of contrary evidence. Poor decisions due to these biases have been found in political and organizational contexts.

> *Be always sure you're right, THEN GO AHEAD!*
> —Davy Crockett

Living in an austere environment *will* be tough! You will likely face many of the following stressors:

- Fear
- Fatigue
- Extreme Cold
- Extreme Heat
- Pain (Physical and emotional)
- Hunger
- Thirst
- Loneliness
- Boredom
- Injury/illness
- Violence

Fear

We humans have an innate fear of the unknown or unfamiliar. By subjecting ourselves to training that rips us out of our known reality, we can, over time, make the unknown familiar. This is the basic premise of military boot camps. If you can't swim, you naturally fear water because it is an unknown environment. You don't possess the skills to survive in an aquatic environment and you know it.

If someone grabs the non-swimmer and suddenly throws them in the water, fear and panic naturally take command. However, when the same treatment is visited upon one who is competent at swimming, there would be a momentary shock, but after this they default to their training and begin treading water. Training builds confidence; our skills are the safety net that catches us when we fall. Confidence and knowledge conquer fear.

Fatigue

Living on the land is hard work and the work of the survivor is never done. Building and constantly improving upon your shelter is laborious work. The quest for water and fuel never ends. As you constantly construct devices to procure food, you most likely do so with little caloric intake. Security must be in place around the clock and will be compounded in a hostile environment. Your work will never be finished. There is no finish line.

The combination of limited calories and sleep deprivation can be crippling, especially if you find yourself alone and unsupported when bad things happen. It is a good practice to subject yourself to these stressors before gameday. Only then will you know how you personally will perform. We're all different, so grab your backpack and go for a camping trip. The objective of this exercise is to take no food, plan on staying awake the entire time. This can be done alone or as a team. Aim for a duration of forty-eight to seventy-two hours. You will quickly learn a lot about yourself.

The romance never lives up to the reality. The romance of living in the woods while sitting at home watching survival videos on YouTube will soon fall away when you actually do it. You cannot feel the heat, cold, tiredness, hunger and desperation. No one shows their failures and in the real world, there will be many.

Extreme Cold

Cold temperatures, especially when combined with wind and rain, can kill a human animal in short order. Because of this, I highly recommend that you make shelter construction and fire creation your first training priorities. Mastery of these two skills is essential to your survival.

Extreme Heat

You can generally create an acceptably warm environment no matter how cold your surroundings may be. However, you can only remove so many clothes until people begin to feel awkward. Proper clothing, a wide brimmed hat and above all, hydration, are key. Taking shelter in the day and moving at night are essential in the roasting regions.

Pain

If you are experiencing pain, that means you are still alive. Embrace it! The source of your pain may be physical injury. You may face emotional pain from having seen or having done violence. Embrace it. Pain has never killed anyone, and no one is coming to save you. Just because you're hurting doesn't mean you can quit; keep on clawing and crawling until things go dark. History is full of amazing people doing seemingly impossible things. Study them and store their experiences away in your mind for inspiration. If they can do it, you can do it. We humans are amazing beasts.

Hunger

In modern western cultures, few of us are in danger of starvation. In fact, most folks that I have seen are carrying around onboard reserves that would last for several weeks. In short term survival, food is rarely a priority. However, in the long emergency that I foresee, food will be critical. As a human, food is one of your most basic dependencies.

Few of us in the modern world have known true hunger. I have personally experienced starvation level hunger a few times. Staying super hydrated and rationing my energetic expenditures carried me through. Escaping into your mind to transcend your current plight is a good thing. That's why it's important to live for today, to create those memories that someday may be your only source of strength.

Humans can exist on much less than you think. A mouthful of

sustenance can realign the trajectory of your crashing morale. Learn to forage, learn to trap. Insects are delicious and more easily obtained than the gazelle.

Thirst

The first question I usually ask myself is, *where is the water?* Water is the blood of the earth; without it, we perish. All solid planning efforts and any good kit will enable you to locate sources of water, render it safe to drink and carry it with you. It has often been said, *ration sweat, not water.*

Loneliness

Human beasts are social creatures. Isolation can reduce a person to a state of madness. For this reason, it has been used as a form of punishment in societies and prisons the world over.

The best way to harden yourself against this is to forge yourself into the type of person that can work in a team or go it alone if need be. Strive to be one who can interact with people and enjoy their company without a feeling of dependence upon them. The stronger you are as an individual, the more well-rounded your skills, the better enabled you will be to exist in solitude should fate dictate that as your course.

No one is coming to save you. There is no help but self-help. If you are spiritually inclined, all the better. Personally speaking, I have never felt more alone than when in the company of others.

Boredom

Once things stabilize, and they will, for better or worse, boredom will set in. This will be your new normal. Humans are creatures of habit; we tend to establish patterns of life. Daily chores quickly become mundane. We have all experienced boredom. This boredom is magnified in austere conditions because our options to remedy it are few.

We normally distract ourselves with social media or some electronic entertainment. Some use alcohol or other substances as an escape. Many people are on mind-altering medications to help them cope with life. When these forms of escape and distraction are no longer available, you are left with only the things that you carry in your mind. Transcendental thinking, visualization and your imagination can see you through. You must learn to create your own fun, even if only within the space of your mind. Children are masterful at this. Endeavor to find humor in all things.

Boredom will be most severe for the lone survivor while groups can use conversation and storytelling, a nearly lost art, to momentarily escape the monotony. I once had the misfortune to be trapped in a very small shelter for five days with zero food. The wind was near hurricane force, the rain fell in torrents. I curled up in a ball and slept as much as possible to conserve calories and pass the time. I recited poetry and other passages I'd committed to memory. I took mental vacations. I pondered the true meaning of life; yielding to my thoughts, I allowed them to carry me away. Nothing lasts forever. Eventually this storm will end, I told myself. It did. They always do.

Injury/Illness

A substantial injury or illness can be crippling to a team. The psychological impact can be severe, especially if the victim is someone you know and love. If definitive medical care is not an option, you will feel totally helpless after you have done what you can with what's available to ease the suffering. In this life there are worse things than death. Prevention is the key; great care should be taken to avoid injury and illness. However, it will likely happen at some point. Monitor yourself and your companions constantly. Have the best medical kit and training possible. These must be in place *before* the need arises. I have personally felt a life slip away as I did all that I could to prevent it. It changes you, and the images will remain with you the rest of your life.

Violence

Interpersonal violence has been part of the human scene as long as there have been people. In the midst of a crisis, the violence will certainly intensify. You will do and see things done that will leave an indelible mark on your soul.

If you have the moral high ground, the mental, emotional and spiritual impact will be lessened. There is no shame in defending the lives of your loved ones, or your own. There is no shame in protecting the defenseless from the merciless. Just be sure you're right, then do what you must. Self-preservation is a natural right. There will be an aftermath though, so monitor yourself and each other. Talk about it. If you hold it in, it will either consume you from within or reach untenable pressures and explode. Neither of these eventualities is optimal.

Final Thoughts on Psychology

Your victory or defeat will be determined by your mindset. Your perspective shapes your reality. The old saying, *the best way to eat a cow is one bite at a time*, has served me well when faced with an overwhelming situation. Instead of becoming paralyzed by the magnitude of our dilemma, we should simply prioritize the situation. It's not uncommon to face multiple crises simultaneously. I often ask myself, *what will kill me first?* I then formulate a plan. Taking a step-by-step approach enables you to focus and begin working on the solution. This approach defeats the tendency towards becoming overwhelmed or ineffective. Once the first thing is settled, move on to the next and then the next, until you have obtained a satisfactory outcome.

Often, people have won or lost the battle before the fight has even begun. They have either defeated themselves in their own minds or they have made a conscious decision to prevail, come what may.

I measure my success not in days, but in pieces of days. I often focus on my next immediate task. If boiling water is the order of the now, I enter it fully, excluding all else. The past will never be recaptured, the future may never be ours; here and now is all we really have, moment to moment. When we choose to live in the now, we forgive the past and have no attachment to the future. It's a form of stoicism. It just is.

When I was young, there was a popular saying, *go with the flow.* Well, I've come to realize that there really is a flow! We can tap into it at any moment we choose. My very best friend is eighty plus years old. Joseph F. White is his name and he often reminds me that, *worry is a wasted emotion and serves no useful purpose.* He would be right! Most of our fears never become reality.

We are often prisoners in walls of our own making, the architects of our own misery. Perspective really does dictate our reality! There have been moments in my life that I thought I would not take another step, yet I did. I took in a deep breath and gave it all I had and pressed on, and so can you! I have adopted a mantra, and I repeat it in those moments I think I may die, *not dead, can't quit! Not dead, can't quit! Not dead, can't quit!* I will push on to the next thing, and the next, until there is no life force left in me; this is my creed! If my heart still beats and my lungs still function, my creator is not finished with me, and I will not be finished. It's just that simple.

Why do you want to survive so badly anyway? What's your purpose? Your children? Your lover? Hockey? Whatever it is, cling to that! No one knows what they are truly capable of, not even themselves. Never quit!

2 - The Village

The lone wolf will soon be the dead wolf.
—Alan Kay

S INCE MAN'S ARRIVAL ON THE earth, we have lived in communities, tribes or groups. Early man simply could not survive on his own. He needed the help of his kith and kin. As hunter-gatherers, early man was highly dependent on seasonal patterns and having the ability to capitalize on the abundance of the moment. Working alone, a single individual or even a band of two or three, simply would not have the manpower to accomplish all the tasks needed.

In Sebastian Junger's book, *Tribe*, the author relates several stories of European settlers of the American frontier that, after being captured by indigenous peoples and subsequently freed by their colonial brethren, would many times refuse to return to *civilized* society. The moral restrictions and disparity of wealth in western society were less palatable than the egalitarian societies of the natives.

While I am not going to try and promote the strength or weakness of either of these forms of society, we can draw some conclusions. It is interesting to consider that people born and raised in a western society, taken captive and then given the opportunity to return to it, would prefer to remain in the *uncivilized* society instead.

The indigenous peoples operated on the principle of personal freedom and obligation to the tribe. Personal property was generally limited to what one could carry on their person or possibly on a horse. It also limited the ability of any one member of the tribe to accumulate any more food or other commodity than others of the tribe. Taking more than your fair share of food could lead to summary execution.

While the punishments of greed may seem extreme to our modern eyes, it served man well. The old saying, *many hands make for light work* is the guiding principle of the tribe. By the tribe working as a collective, they could ensure enough food was gathered, processed and stored away for winter. The great bison hunts of the American plains are a perfect example of this.

The hunters, or braves, would range ahead of the rest of the village that was carrying their camps along with them. When the young men found the beasts, the slaughter would begin. This wasn't a lopsided endeavor, and many perished in pursuit of the most valuable food source of the tribes. As the animals were killed, the women would come behind and begin the butchering. Each person in these societies had their place. They each had tasks they were expected to fulfill.

But it wasn't only the meat the natives were after when hunting this ultimate big game. The skins were used for everything from tipi coverings to clothes and bedding. The bones were used for tools and decoration and many of the animal's organs held magical powers in their beliefs and were used in both ceremony and medicine.

While the indigenous peoples didn't pursue individual wealth, they did pursue honor. This was accomplished through feats of hunting or in mortal combat. One did not rise through the ranks of native society because they had more money than their fellows. Instead, they were judged on their character; and the worst thing one could be called was a coward.

And while the tribes enjoyed games of chance and skill, cheating was nearly as universally despised as being lazy and not carrying one's weight for the betterment of the tribe. Contrary to the beliefs common to the era, and still today, native women were not slaves. Once accepted into the tribe (this is also true of captives who could become full tribal members with all the inherent rights), they were free to live their lives according to their choosing. They chose who to marry and decided when they were no longer married.

On the whole, tribal life was one that afforded the native considerable free time. This can be seen in the numerous pieces of art they fashioned.

From headbands to jewelry, the natives had time to spend making something that offered nothing to their daily survival. Jewelry couldn't help in the hunting and paintings didn't ensure your tipi was warm in the winter. It was the collective effort of free persons working in concert that allowed the tribe as a whole to thrive and the individual to pursue personal pleasures. Now, I know someone is going to throw the red flag of socialism on this play. But there is a profound difference between freely working with others that you have both familial and tribal ties to for the betterment of the group as a whole and forced western ideals of socialism.... in the words of Marx, *from each according to his ability, to each according to his need.* No native was compelled to perform acts for the betterment of another at the cost to himself. It wasn't until Europeans arrived on the scene that this sort of thing began; and it was usually with the native on the losing end of the deal.

I begin with this example to demonstrate just how far we've moved from those early days. In the modern world, each person is out for themselves and maybe their immediate family. Family ties quickly fray as members drift away from one another and seldom come in contact, save the occasional reunion. This sort of tribal loyalty is still here today in many places on Earth. Familial bonds are still strong, and they are the cornerstone of their societies. They still exist as a tribe and the tribe comes before all else.

In tribal societies, disputes are generally settled by the elders who are respected and shown the deference they deserve. Once an elder makes a ruling on a disagreement, it is usually accepted and there is no more discussion on the matter. Compare that to the litigious society we live in today. No man, woman or single family can go it alone. You need a tribe, militant homeowners association, group, whatever you want to call it. If you haven't already begun building yours, get started today! Just like you, dear reader who is thinking this is impossible, there are many thousands more thinking the same thing. You just need to learn how to find them.

Hands down, assembling a tribe is the hardest thing you will do when it comes to your survival planning. It's not the latest gadget and you can't buy it on Amazon. It takes time, years in most cases, to find those people that you can trust. Trust them you must for you are trusting them with you most valuable possession, your life and the lives of those you love most. Those of your tribe str going to be to be doing the you, placing that ultimate trust in your hands.

People want easy solutions. They want to buy things that they can look at, step back and say, *I'm doing something to be prepared*. When it comes to community, that simply doesn't work. You have to put in the hard work, network, get to know those around you. What are their skills? What are their liabilities? What are they bringing to the table? It is also best to see them at their worst. In a crisis situation, do they rise to the occasion, or simply fall apart?

Not every member of your community needs to be a tactical ninja commando either. I'd take an old woman that knew how to garden in my tribe over three of those guys. A dentist and/or doctor are indispensable. Someone with engineering skills, chemistry and carpentry skills would go a long way to improving your group's survival rate.

A community is a diverse collection of skilled individuals. Consider the medieval village. There was the farmer that grew the wheat. He would take his bounty to the thresher who separated the grain from the chaff. This cleaned grain would then be taken to the miller that milled the grains the farmers brought to town in exchange for a share of the bounty. No money changed hands. There was the blacksmith who fashioned all manner of iron implements and was often paid in commodities. These societies existed as symbiotic relationships, each individual doing their part for the betterment of the whole.

In times of conflict, these same people came together to defend what they'd created and worked so hard to cultivate. And when things escalated to the point of combat, you knew the men standing at your side. You knew you could depend on them, and they on you. For not only were you fighting for your family's survival, but also your brothers to either side. You knew their wives, their children and there was a good chance they were kin to some degree.

Let's contrast that with today's society. Most people live in cities in apartments, human warehouses. Seldom do they know their neighbors and they feel absolutely no allegiance to them. Nor do they know the grocer where they purchase their food, as they do not grow or raise any of it themselves now. Instead of the food that nourishes their bodies growing within sight of their homes, it's transported from around the globe and delivered to them in varying degrees of readiness.

Modern men, and women, spend more hours of their lives with people they have very little in common with in pursuit of the almighty dollar than with their own tribe. They must travel farther from their family units. The idea of a tribe having died a long time ago, they toil their days away at the behest of others, often surrounded by people with which they have no real connection. No religious, racial, political and certainly not familial connections. In essence, they have no shared experience, except that of the workplace.

A contrast can be made here with prison. People with vast differences are forced into a box and expected to live together. Here, a different form of hierarchy forms. It has nothing to do with experience or respect. It usually comes in the form of physical dominance. In the workplace, it's those that can best manipulate the corporate game that get ahead. Take these same people that excel in the cubical farm and place them in a real farm, and they would crumble under both the physical and mental demands.

However, all is not lost. We need to be forming our own tribes. We need to be surrounding ourselves with people that we know we can count on no matter how bad things get. In a perfect world, your tribe would be local to you. Having a tribal member 400 miles away does you little good when an emergency arises. I'm not saying it's a bad idea to have a broad network in place. You never know when you may have to evacuate your current location and having a place to go is invaluable. But for day-today life, you need men and women around you that will stand with you in the face of the most heinous of circumstances. Because if they will stand shoulder to shoulder with you as the beast bears down upon you, then they will certainly be there when the roof needs patching, or the garden needs tending.

The creation of your tribe is both the most important and difficult thing you will undertake in your prepping. And for good reason, it's that important. By now, you're probably asking, how do I go about finding these stalwart souls I can bond with? The answer is, you should have started five years ago. If you didn't, then today is the next best day to start.

Start by probing their thought processes through casual conversation. Talk politics, often a taboo, and listen more than you speak. Share stories of growing up to get a feel for their life experiences. Engage in outdoor activities together, camping, fishing, hunting and the like. See how they perform in adverse conditions. But do not discount them out of hand if they perform poorly. If Bob doesn't like to camp but is a hell of a HAM radio operator, he is still a major asset.

Look for diversity of skills. Having ten guys that all like to go to a gun range and punch holes in targets does not mean you have two rifle squads that can take on the world. As mentioned earlier, people that can grow food, raise livestock, engineers, carpenters and many other skill sets are far more valuable. If you have to use a rifle every day, you will not live long enough for those other things to matter. Going to the gun should be a last resort, always.

I have a good friend that has been around the world. This man is a warrior and has spent his entire life in that pursuit. He's quite skilled in the arts of combat. He has a saying he likes to share, (said in a British accent) *I carry a pistol to remind meself not to use me pistol.* Just because you have a gun doesn't mean it should always be your first choice. As a matter of fact, it should be your last, when all other options have failed.

Once you've started to assemble your tribe, begin having group events. Start soft, maybe bowling or meeting at the lake for a BBQ and work your way up to training events. Every group should meet once a month at the minimum, and weekly would be better. This is where those members with hard skills can begin training the rest of the group. If no one in your group is highly skilled in the use of weapons, bring a qualified trainer in to teach. Split the cost up to make it affordable for all. Take a HAM radio class and get licensed, then get the equipment and use it. And the list goes on, learn as many skills as possible.

There is one surefire way to build unit cohesion. That is after all what you're doing, building a small unit. It's simple it its concept but can be a little harder in its implementation. A primary component of this is mutual suffering. I know your mouth is hanging open and you're questioning my sanity but hear me out. Ask any combat vet or back-woods hunter about the trips they remember the most. More often than not, they will regale you with a tale of when the weather was horrific, they were cold, miserable, hungry and people were trying to kill them. Many of the combat vets will tell you they'd made peace with the fact they were going to die there and then.

It's not the good times, the soft times that bring people together. It's those times when each man was tested to his limit and had to rely on the strength of his brothers to see him through that left a mark he'll never forget. For each man knows that if not for the brothers around him, he would have given up. The only reason he didn't was because he didn't want to let them down. Note, he wasn't concerned about let-ting himself down. That's easy to do, to simply give up. But he couldn't live with himself if he let his brothers down. That is a tribe.

And you can replicate this same experience yourself. Plan a group outing when the weather is forecasted to be absolutely miserable, the worse, the better. Plan to spend three days suffering through this. Will it be fun? No. Will you want to quit? Absolutely. But the men and women that come out the other side will be people that you know you can count on. Nothing builds bonds like mutual suffering. Any member of a tribe should be able to put out the call for help and the rest of the tribe should be willing to drop whatever they are doing to come to their aid.

I have members of my tribe that I would follow to the ends of the earth should they call. That's how strong these bonds should be. And right now, you have a tribe to build.

3 - E.D.C.
Every Day Carry

When the dust settles, only the prepared will survive.
—Angery American

THE ACRONYM EDC REFERS TO the term *Every Day Carry*. These are the items we habitually take with us as a matter of daily course. For the uninitiated, a cell phone, car keys and credit card may suffice.

However, these items fall short in the quest to sustain our lives when the bad things happen. A good EDC kit should better enable us to satisfy the following requirements:

- Water
- Shelter
- Fire
- Food Procurement
- Signaling
- Navigation
- Medical
- Personal Security

Note: **The smaller the items, the smaller the kit. The smaller the kit, the more likely it is that you will actually carry it on your person daily!**

When kits become bulky or cumbersome, they tend to be left behind in the vehicle or the home. The term EDC implies carrying the items in the pockets or the belt, never separate in a bag or pack. Those with military training will recognize it as first-line gear.

I realize that some may face individual limitations trying to implement all the recommendations set forth in this chapter. For example, some of you may not be able to dress in such a way that would facilitate the carriage of all the items mentioned. Formal business attire is noticeably lacking in pockets. Students obviously cannot carry firearms or edged implements, neither can employees of a courthouse, Federal building or most corporations. My goal is to simply show what I typically carry and why. Take the ideas that work for you and dismiss the rest. Your location will also dictate what is carried.

Potable water is often taken for granted in our society. In an emergency or natural disaster, we quickly see its true worth. To successfully meet your hydration needs, you will require the following:

- A source
- A container
- A means of rendering it safe to drink

I can't help with the source, that part is up to you—be sure to choose wisely.

A container by its very nature can be difficult to conceal because it occupies a physical space that usually cannot be altered. However, technology has blessed us with some options thanks to the advent of plastics. Some advocate the use of condoms but, they only work when there is a flow sufficient enough to stretch them. I once carried them in my kit but quickly discovered they were inadequate. The level of care required to implement them rendered them more a false sense of security than an asset.

One option is the highly concealable plastic bag, such as the Platypus and Whirl-Pak bags. The Whirl-Pak bags are great for small kits as they can be rolled or folded to fit in survival tins or other kit containers. They have a pleated gusset on the bottom; however, they will not stand when full. They are rugged enough for austere conditions and will hold up immensely better than the condom.

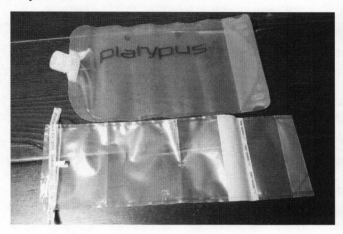

The Platypus bag (top) and the Whirl-Pak bag.

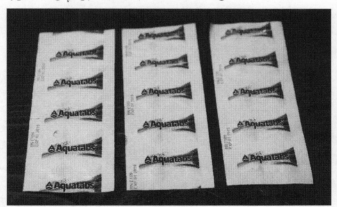

Aquatabs water purification tablets.

The Platypus bag is a great method for transporting water, either pre or post treatment. They are much more durable than the Whirl-Pak bags, but this comes with a couple of costs. First, they do not pack up as small as the Whirl-Pak. Second, they have a hard mouth on them.

This can be both a liability and an asset. It is a liability in that it's a hard point that can be prone to wear, an asset in that this small threaded opening will fit on some filters, such as the Sawyer Mini.

Most commercially available water purification tablets will do. I prefer those portioned into small packages as they are more readily concealed than small round bottles.

Another advantage of using tablets is the fact that I can scoop up some water and keep moving, letting the tablets go to work while I walk. This option is good for use in situations where time is of the essence. Moreover, if I am trying to avoid human contact, less time at the water source translates to less chance of discovery. Additionally, tablets enable me to keep my use of fire to a minimum. The limiting factor concerning tablets is that you will eventually deplete your supply.

Concerning shelter, carrying items such as a knife, wire saw, and mylar blanket can make the task much easier and more efficient.

Fire is a versatile companion. Anyone serious about survival will never be without three reliable ignition sources and some emergency tinder. Also, your knife and wire saw will assist you in gathering and processing fuel.

The tinder straw is an essential part of your survival kit.

Packing soaked cotton into straw.

A small ferrocerium rod should be carried in every kit. I usually have two on my person at all times. It is also advisable to keep a couple of brightly colored lighters in your pocket. A Fresnel lens is also a handy item. With this, you can focus the rays of the sun to create a fire. You can also use it as a visual aid should you misplace your reading glasses. They are inexpensive and take up little space.

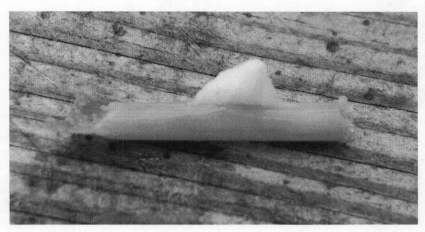

A tinder straw cut open to expose the inner fiber. Be sure to fluff them up before attempting to ignite the straw.

While it requires sufficient sunlight, the Fresnel lens is a great backup fire starter.

Brass wire has many uses, snares for trapping among them.

Food really isn't a top priority in a short-term situation. It is wise though to carry a few items for fishing and trapping. Such activities can also keep the survivor occupied to better cope psychologically.

Snares are a great way to grab some groceries. Practice making and using them before your life depends on it. Wire for snares can be hard to come by, thus it should be carried. Bank line is an excellent survival cordage and takes up less room than the ubiquitous parachute cord (550). I live in an area with plentiful lakes and streams, so I always carry a small fishing kit.

A few meal replacement bars stuffed into your pocket may be a good idea. If nothing else, it will keep the kids quiet . . . for a minute. Any serious survivor will have studied at least a few edible plants readily available in the immediate environment. Don't be squeamish about bugs, slugs, worms and insects. They are easy to catch and full of goodness; cook 'em though, parasites are not your friend.

Signaling

In my experience while giving feedback to students, I have noticed an overall lack of signaling material in their survival kits. While visiting Africa, on two separate occasions, the need to signal (communicate) arose. In the first case, an Afrikaner, a Bushman and I had tracked

Right, the VS-17 Panel is an internationally recognized visual signal.

Below, Alan waving a signal panel.

down an animal that we were hunting. The animal lay before us as the sun was going to sleep. The sounds of Hyenas and other beasts drew nearer and nearer as the sky darkened. Both my companions were visibly uneasy. Being new to Africa, I was seriously concerned about being consumed by those beasts that patrolled the night. So, I began pulling out my pocket survival kit to build a fire. Shortly thereafter, using hand signs, the Bushman indicated an approaching vehicle. I stood, facing in the direction that he had given. I then withdrew my flashlight

Using a signal mirror.

(aka, torch to our British brethren) and began sending pulses of light across the Kalahari. Simultaneously, I grasped my whistle, placed it in my mouth and began sending three round bursts toward my intended target.

Rapidly thereafter, the bouncing lights of my Toyota savior appeared on the horizon! I was relieved! We were all relieved! Upon arrival at my location, the occupants of the vehicle stated that they had both seen and heard my distress call. Therein lies the key! Audible and visual! By day and by night!

Small button compass.

Once again, as the sun prepared to slumber, we found ourselves near a pan (this is a body of water during the wet season) for a sundowner (the practice of drinking with friends as the sun sets). We were unable to communicate our position by means of conversation on the radio. So, I had the man holding the radio tell our companions to switch the vehicle off and listen for a whistle. I blew the whistle with three strong blasts, a brief pause between each. The disembodied voice came back, "yep, got you mate, that was a proper toot-toot whistle!" A $2.00 whistle prevailed where modern digital communications failed. Low tech always works. Carry one.

A brightly colored piece of cloth can be tied to a pole and used as a daytime visual signal.

A small signal mirror can be seen over a great distance. Other uses include conducting visual inspections of your body to remove ticks and leeches, or to assess an injury when alone.

A small button compass takes up little room and will aid you in direction-finding and should be a part of every kit.

Medical

You can suddenly find yourself or another in medical distress. Preparation is essential. This preparation should come in the form of training primarily and material secondarily. I make it a daily practice to carry a tourniquet. When a tourniquet is needed, they are needed right now! Trying to improvise one on the fly will be a futile effort, potentially resulting in someone's death. Not to mention, they are extremely difficult to

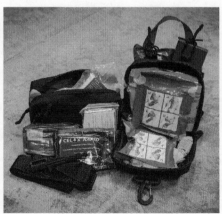

A quality trauma kit should contain all the necessary materials to handle arterial bleeding, tension pneumothorax and airway control.

self-apply. Some are more easily carried than others. Find the one that works for you.

Are they breathing? Is there a pulse? What do you do? *You must get training now!* A book won't do! Hands-on training! Get some!

Personal Security

Security is always excessive until it's not enough.
—Robbie Sinclair

People are always potentially dangerous. Animals can be dangerous if you violate the rules of the bush. Blessed is the survivor that is in possession of a weapon and is proficient in its use. A stick, knife, shovel or bare hands can be used. You must have a weapon. For our purpose, weapons will fall into three categories.

1. Edged (Knives, hatchet, etc.)

2. Impact (Club, flashlight, etc.)

3. Projectile (Firearm, slingshot, etc.)

No human beast endeavoring to subsist even a single day would be found wanting of cold, hard, steel! Your knife is your life.

Sometimes, legalities get in the way and you may be forced to repurpose daily items into an arrowhead or *shank* (improvised prison weapon). That's not living your best life. When legal and possible, carry a quality knife. A full tang knife is always best, but a folder is more socially palatable. And it will be easier to defend to a jury of your peers should it be pressed into service in defense of your life. Knives are tools and tools require maintenance. For this reason, I carry a sharpening stone the size of a credit card that fits in my wallet.

A good flashlight will serve as a perfect impact weapon. You should always carry a flashlight for multiple reasons. Signaling and target identification among them. Get the brightest light you can in the form factor that works for you. Light in itself can be a weapon. Not to mention, most flashlights are TSA approved.

A reliable handgun is one of the best self-defense tools. The ability to project force and influence over distance can really tip the odds in your favor. You *must* receive reality-based training from a competent instructor. The focus should be fighting with the pistol not just hitting the targets. A pistol is like a good pair of shoes, they either fit or they don't. Find the one that fits you. The pistol is part of an overall system; it is incomplete without a quality belt and holster. Additionally, we recommend the carrying of at least one reload.

Recommended reading on the carrying of a pistol: ***Clandestine Pistol Carry*** by John Mosby. We highly recommend Tactical Response for firearms training.

Pistol, holster and reload.

4 - Shelter

Our houses are such unwieldy property that we are of-
ten imprisoned rather than housed in them.
—Henry David Thoreau, *Walden*

I N OUR CURRENT MODERN LIVES, we are often within the confines of some artificial climate-controlled shelter. Rarely are we
subjected to the vicissitudes of nature for extended periods. Let's
examine an average day in the modern world. We awaken between layers of clean, dry bedding, safely encapsulated inside our home.

If we deem it too cold or too warm, we simply adjust the thermo-
stat. Before entering the shower, we select the perfect water temperature. Upon exiting our scrub session, we lay hold of a nice dry towel,
dress in clean, dry clothes and make our way to the kitchen where food
and drink await in sufficient quantity, held at the desired temperature.
We turn the tap; clean water comes out ready to use. Magic.

Now we enter the garage, which is a shelter for our vehicle that
is more secure a dwelling than many people on earth will ever call
home. We enter our vehicle and with the press of a button, up goes the
garage door. The engine turns over and we proceed on our journey as
we easily command the temperature within by means of switches and
knobs; wow, even the seats are heated or cooled. A car is just a shelter
with wheels.

Finally, we arrive at the parking area. Here, we find ourselves in great peril, open sky! No walls! With a latte in one hand and an umbrella in the other, we move with a sense of urgency as the wind begins to blow and the raindrops fall. Whew! We arrive safe and dry, that was a close one!

Now, we enter the large sturdy shelter of an office building. Fatigued from our sprint, we step into the elevator, which is a mini shelter that renders travel by means of stairs and our feet obsolete. At last, we arrive at our cubicle which shelters us from the prying eyes and distractions of others.

When the workday is done, we return to our shelter on wheels and transfer ourselves to yet another shelter location wherein we find shelves neatly stocked with boxes and supplies. We place the desired items into a cart with wheels which relieves us of the physical exertion of carrying these burdensome supplies, which we spent no time or energy to produce.

On the way back to our primary shelter [home], we begin to feel the first waves of hunger. Never mind the fact that the backseat is mounded in plastic bags bursting with food, we pull into a drive-through and communicate with the ones preparing yet more food by means of an electronic box and retrieve it through a window, all without leaving the relative safety and comfort of our shelter with wheels. At long last, we return to our home, exhausted. The exhaustion we feel is more spiritual, emotional, and mental than physical.

When we find ourselves in the open, on the land, we quickly discover that nothing is ready-made or convenient. Often, the only immediate shelter we have is our clothing. All else must be constructed with our own hands. Statistically speaking, exposure to the elements is one of the most common ways people die outdoors. The average human today has devolved to the point where they can no longer sustain their own life in their natural habitat, the earth. The first step to remedy this condition is the ability to create shelter.

I have seen many a student feverishly laboring away at building a grand structure. In terms of survival, this is folly. We must first understand that a proper shelter for survival has to be more like a sleeping bag and less like a house. This is true for several reasons. First, the object of a shelter is to maintain the temperature of the body so that you may survive. Second, with a smaller shelter, less material will be required in its construction. Thus, less time and energy are required of the builder, which means fewer precious calories are burned. Primitive shelter construction is laborious, demanding many hours of intense work, so the smaller, the better.

Before beginning the actual construction of a shelter, it is best to take a deep breath and consider a few things. A good shelter is akin to a successful restaurant, it's all about location. If we place our shelter too close to water, we may find insects and unwanted animal encounters to be a problem. Also, the noise of rushing water may drown out other sounds like the voices of rescuers or approaching danger. If we locate our humble abode too far away from water, we may find that walking back and forth to obtain water is an inefficient use of our time and energy.

Where are our food resources? Just like our considerations regarding water, too close is bad and too far is also not optimal. As we inspect the ground, do we see that we are in a game trail? Do we see the coming and going of dangerous insects? Is the scene safe? Are dead trees or falling rocks a potential hazard? Is this area likely to become suddenly flooded?

Are there suitable materials with which to build this shelter? Do they exist in sufficient quantity? All shelters are largely decided for us by the location in which the need arises. In one location, stones and moss may be the primary material. In another, sticks and leaves or even palm fronds and grass may be the chief resources. Shelter construction is largely intuitive. You are limited only by the materials at hand, the laws of physics and your own imagination. Many problems can be avoided by doing our mental homework before breaking a sweat. As I do a 360° scan of a potential shelter site, I ask myself, "What already looks like a shelter?

For example, it is far easier to take a rocky overhang and make it home than it would be to begin from scratch. Shelter building is a skill, and like all skills, it must be practiced before it is needed. There is no substitute for an actual experiential frame of reference. A good shelter will guard the occupant against wind, rain, and above all, conduction. Conduction, lying directly upon the cold, hard ground will literally suck the life from your body. Conduction kills. A shelter without a mattress is no shelter at all! I once spent 55 days in a simple shelter, a lean-to. I improved upon it almost daily, mainly the bed, for a period of two weeks, adding additional grass at every opportunity.

For another perspective, let's consider the habitat of a homeless person in an urban setting. The urban survivor builds a shelter from available materials such as cardboard, newspaper, plastic and used pallets. This shelter stops wind and rain. It also insulates the occupant without a dependence on fire. Most importantly, the savvy city survivalist will place as much material as possible between the body and the cold earth. Usually, layers of cardboard achieve this. Commonly, a layer of plastic is placed first on the ground to prevent moisture from finding its way into the cardboard. GENIUS! The homeless have lessons to teach us. Naturally, the question arises, "Is it possible to actually be homeless?" I say no. Wherever I am, there is my home. Survival is largely your mindset. How you perceive and interact with your circumstances will decide the outcome.

Primitive shelter construction is one of those skills best learned through hands-on experience. We *highly* recommend seeking training from a competent instructor. Books and YouTube videos cannot convey the physical effort, the importance of safe tool handling and the sheer volume of material required. Every student we've ever trained comes out with an entirely different view on the subject and a newfound appreciation for items such as a sleeping bag and tarp! Carrying these items in your pack or vehicle relieves you of the profound burden that is shelter construction. Preparation really is the key.

5 - Water, Blood of the Earth

Also known as the official soft drink of planet earth.
Or, if you're from Appalachia, unrefined liquor.

THE SURFACE OF THIS ROCK we call home, Earth, is covered in approximately seventy-one percent water. The human body is about sixty percent water. But it gets a little more interesting. Your brain is about seventy-three percent water, as is your heart. Think about that for a moment. Nearly three quarters of the organs where most people believe the soul resides, the brain and the heart, are water. Ever wonder why you have that headache after a night of drinking? Not that we would know, but we've heard stories about it. Or when dehydration sets in, the first place you notice it is with a headache? There's a reason.

Water is life. Without it there is no life. In physics, cold is defined as the absence of heat. The natural state of our universe is cold. It takes a source of heat, a star, to generate that warmth. Think of water in the same manner. Water is life and in the absence of it, there is no life. As a human, you must consume water every day. Every drop of water that you take in you will later expel. It doesn't go into your body and remain there, it's constantly recycled.

There is no more or less water on this planet now than there has ever been. And we're not going to get into the arguments of icy meteors crashing into the earth. Every drop of water you drink has, at some point in the past, been consumed and passed by another living creature.

Now, that's not to say that all water is still in the same form it once was, its pure form. Water today takes on many forms, much of which is so polluted that it is essentially useless. Chemicals are dumped daily by the tens of thousands of gallons into our waterways, oceans and lakes. The one thing we need more than any other on this planet to survive, we appear to be bent on destroying.

All this must be kept in mind by the survivor. Any source of surface water must be considered contaminated and the survivor must know the various ways of dealing with the potential contaminants. In areas with little to no human contaminants, the animal kingdom does a fine job on its own. Giardia and cryptosporidium are examples of the various parasites commonly found in surface water. Luckily, there are easy ways to prevent these bugs from wreaking havoc on your GI tract.

Water Treatment Methods

Depending on the contaminants present, the approach to treatment varies. Sadly, there is no one size fits all. If you are in an area where Giardia is present, you can use chemical treatment, boiling or filtering. Bleach can be used to treat the water by adding two to four drops of liquid odorfree bleach per liter of water. This treated water needs to stand for thirty minutes. If the water is particularly dirty or full of particulates, strain it through a cloth first and go with eight hours.

Iodine is considered a better treatment for Giardia than bleach, though it takes longer. Five drops of 2% tincture of iodine per liter of water is sufficient, requiring the water to sit for up to eight hours to get the job done. Both of these chemical methods also have the disadvantage of the taste that they impart to the water. It will taste like the chemical you used. This can be masked by adding powdered drink mixes, but it will still be there.

Cryptosporidium is another parasite you will face in surface water sources. While initial symptoms are the same, it requires slightly different treatment. Bleach is not an effective treatment for this parasite. While high concentrations of bleach with long durations of exposure can get the job done, the concentration is such that you wouldn't be able to drink the water. Crypto dies at 160 degrees, so boiling is the best method.

Boiling

Boiling is the surest method to ensure parasites are killed off. However, this does nothing for chemical toxins in the water. As mentioned earlier, Crypto dies at 160 degrees and Giardia between 130-145 degrees. At altitudes below two thousand feet, water boils at 212 degrees. So simply bringing your water to a rolling boil will kill anything in it.

There are a lot of different ideas about boiling water above the twothousand-foot mark. The truth is this, above two thousand feet, the temperature at which water boils decreases one degree for every five hundred feet of elevation increase. So, at three thousand feet, your water will boil at 208 degrees. At 7500 feet, water boils around 198 degrees. As you can see, even at these altitudes, simply achieving a rolling boil will kill anything in it. There is no need for a prolonged boil.

Chemical Treatments

Halazone tablets are another commercially available source and easier to carry. Five tablets to a liter of water will be ready to drink in thirty minutes. Just remember to loosen the top of any container you filled directly from the water and slosh your treated water to displace any residual water from the filling process. This is critical or you could still end up with the parasite. Potable Aqua is another brand that is a

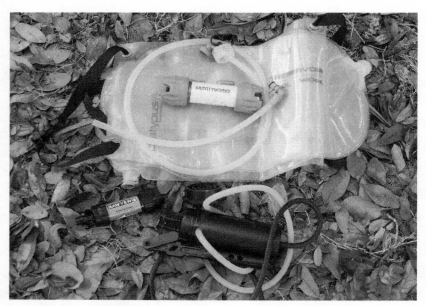

There are a variety of filters on the market. Find the one that works best for you. (*top*, Platypus Gravity Works; *bottom left*, Sawyer Mini; *bottom center*, MSR SweetWater)

two-step process. Two tablets will treat one quart of water. By adding two of the PA+ tablets, the iodine taste in the water will be removed in about three minutes. Just make sure you've allowed proper treatment time before neutralizing the iodine.

Another brand, and one I personally use, is Aquatabs. This is an effervescent tab that looks like an Alka-Seltzer when dropped into water. They take thirty minutes to work and do not have as strong a chlorine taste. All tabs are best used in conjunction with a filter as not all microorganisms are killed by one chemical.

There are numerous water filters on the market now that will get the job done just as well. So long as the filter is .1 micron or less, it will remove the parasites. Most manufacturers also label the filter as removing Giardia. Be sure to read the manufacturer's data sheet provided with the filter to ensure it meets the requirements for your area.

Commercial Filters

There are numerous filter options out there, ranging from pumps to gravity to the popular straw-style filters. All of these have their pros and cons. I prefer pump filters so I can keep all my containers clean as they've only come in contact with filtered water. The gravity filters such as the one by Platypus are great for groups as they filter a large volume of water quickly and with no effort on your part. The straw filters have the added benefit of being able to be cut in-line with the popular hydration systems. This way, you can fill your bladder and rock on, knowing every sip has been filtered. For a more permanent situation, look at the Berkey line of filters. These really are the gold star of filters. I use these exclusively at home for all my drinking water. We live on a well, so all water is filtered. The filters are good for three thousand gallons each. So, a unit with four filters will do twelve thousand gallons of water. And they have the highest level of filtration of anything on the market.

The important thing to remember is that your filter needs to filter particulates down to the .1-micron level. This will remove Giardia and other protozoa. Here again, filters alone will not remove chemical toxins from the water, so be sure of your source. There are filters out there that remove chemical toxins but they are not as portable and generally serve an entire home or building. (Note: The authors are aware of the various filters purported to remove chemical toxins. We've experimented with a few and they did not make us feel warm and fuzzy.)

SODIS

Your last resort is the SODIS method, Solar Water Disinfection Method. This is simple and easy to do, yet time consuming. It's a sad fact that nearly everywhere in the world today we can find plastic bottles. In this case, that's all you need. A plastic beverage bottle less than three inches in diameter is all that's required. Glass will not work as it is a UV filter. Simply fill the bottle with water and place it in direct sunlight for six hours. The UV rays will kill parasites and viruses

The SODIS method is a simple way of reliably treating water. Try and utilize a bottle with the recycle number one on it.

alike. Rotate the bottle periodically to ensure all sides of any debris, or floaters, in the water have been exposed. The bottle becomes a pressure cooker of sorts and this aids in *cooking* off the pathogens. This is a perfectly safe method of water purification, so long as the water doesn't contain toxic compounds. This method has the advantage of not needing a fire or any material other than a plastic bottle. The downside is that it ties you to a fixed location for six hours or more.

The SODIS method is a simple way of reliably treating water. Try and utilize a bottle with the recycle number one on it.

Water is life. Without water there can be no life. Without water there can be no security. Water is so important that it should always be the first consideration when looking at potential bug-out property, retreats or homesteads. If you cannot adequately supply your water needs from your land, you really need to look for a new place. Being forced to leave your secure perimeter to locate water and then attempt to carry it back would be a serious security issue.

You also need the ability to get to that water under any conditions. Is the power out? You do have a hand pump, right? If relying on a creek or other such natural water source, is it seasonal? Are there ground contaminates near the water? Water is sacred; it is the blood of the Earth. Treat it as such.

6 - The Flame

In the beginning of the world, it was Bear who owned Fire. It warmed Bear and his people on cold nights and gave them light when it was dark. Bear and his people carried fire with them wherever they went.
—Opening line of a myth of the Alabama
Tribe, retold by S. E. Schlosser

FIRE IS THE DEAREST COMPANION to a human creature. When you are alone and shivering in a strange land, nothing can quench your thirst for companionship like fire. An often-overlooked facet of fire is the psychological benefit of having a friend. No other single thing can do as much for us as fire can.

In a cold environment, fire can literally determine life or death. It cooks our food, rendering it safe to eat. It enables us to make water safe to drink. With fire, we can signal for rescue. By means of smoke, we can preserve food for later use. With fire, we can shape and temper wood into tools and weapons.

The moment humans learned to create and control fire was the most important technological advancement to date. Without fire, the industrial revolution would not have been possible. The mastery of fire is a human birthright. There is a great sense of peace that comes with knowing you can create fire with your bare hands. I strongly advocate carrying three reliable ignition sources at all times, so that primitive fire making can be avoided. I also believe that every human should master primitive fire as it is the ultimate insurance.

I feel such a strong connection with fire. Every time I spin the stick between my palms, I feel the link to my teachers and my ancestors. It is an unbroken chain back to the very beginning.

Fire has much to teach; patience, forethought, humility and perseverance. It truly is magic. My journey with fire has been long and it continues still. I often feel tears building in my eyes as I teach a group of children about fire for the first time. I love sharing the magic moment when a flame is born. I consider it an indescribable honor to be one of the few who carry the fire.

One of my mentors shared with me that he says the words, "I come humbly," each time he makes a fire. I have adopted this practice and carry on his tradition. Another mentor, Al Cornell, says of fire making, "You have to sneak up on it." Others who have helped me along the fire path are Mark Warren, Russell Cutts, Forest Hillyer, Mike Campbell and Myron Creteney. I think it is important to honor our teachers and I love you all very much.

There is an equation that I think sums up fire making nicely. Proper material + proper technique = fire. No matter the method we use to make fire, material selection is critical. We must acknowledge that there is an intimate connection between the plant kingdom and fire. Botany is the foundation upon which fire is built.

Many a fire has been lost due to a lack of initial preparation. You must prepare your fuel, process your tinder and carve your kit. Then go for it.

The Hand Drill

The hand drill is my favorite friction fire method. From the moment I first saw this technique, it took me several years to reach a decent level of proficiency. That long journey has caused me to cherish this skill as it was hard won. I love the simplicity of this method; it can be tough on the hands though.

One advantage to the hand drill is that no cordage is required. A distant disadvantage is that you will find this method to be very challenging in wet conditions. This is because it lacks the mechanical advantage afforded by methods such as the bow drill.

Once all the required materials have been gathered, begin by warming the wood. It is essential that you use the full length of both hands equally.

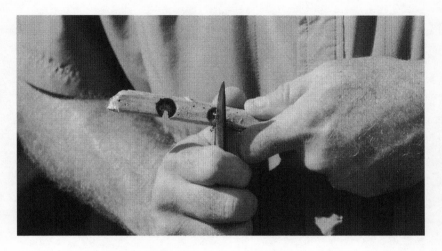

Properly notching the fireboard is important, take your time.

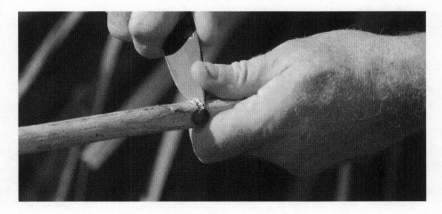

Utilize the "push cut" method to prevent injuries.

Care must be taken when preparing the hand drill. Notice the point is carefully carved and is flat on the end.

The hole for the drill must be "burned" into the fireboard.

Use the entire length of your hands and maintain positive downward pressure. Notice, Alan is using his boot to hold the fireboard securely in place.

Smoke is a good sign! Now's the time to really get after it!

Carefully place your coal into the tinder bundle.

Now breathe
life into
your fire!

The Bow Drill

The bow drill is perhaps the most familiar of the friction fire methods. Many people learn this method first. I did. The bow drill gives us an awesome mechanical advantage. There is a degree of complexity, though, as it requires multiple components, cordage among them. In some situations, cordage can be difficult to obtain. In such a case, you could use your boot laces or sacrifice the edges from a piece of clothing.

The socket, AKA bearing block or hand hold, can also take a bit of creativity and work to produce. Many knives are available with the bow-drill divet built into the handle. Such a device is quite handy. A canteen cup can also be used but you will need a glove or some other insulating material between the cup and your hand.

The Fire Saw

The bamboo fire saw is a beautiful and simple method of friction fire. Everything you require can be found in a single piece of bamboo, including the tinder.

The fire saw is physically demanding, so be ready for the workout. Bamboo is increasingly becoming part of the landscape here in the U.S. Once on an urban survival exercise, I found a picture frame made of bamboo while dumpster diving. I repurposed this into a fire saw. Bamboo furnishings and decorations can be found in many homes and hotels. Primitive techniques can save the day, even in an urban setting. Knowledge is power.

The dry bamboo must be split down the center ideally.

The notch will be cut near a node for added strength.

Now it's all about muscle power!

Tinder

A good tinder bundle is paramount to a successful fire-making session, especially when a friction method is to be used. Dry grasses, tree bark and other plant fibers can be used. You should never pass up an opportunity to collect tinder. Always be ready for your next fire! In the mountains where I live, the inner bark of the tulip poplar has become my staple tinder. In a more tropical setting, the "monkey fur" that is found against the trunk of the cabbage palm between old fronds is the best tinder available.

Your tinder can be refined by rubbing it between your palms or against a tree or rock. This exposes more surface area of the material. Take the time to process your tinder thoroughly; it will pay dividends. Great care should be taken to find the driest tinder available and to keep it dry.

The coal you will produce should be viewed as a newborn baby. The tinder bundle is the warm safe place that you have prepared to receive this delicate new life, so that you may nurse it into its flaming destiny.

Not all tinder is created equally. I typically separate tinder into three categories. Primary, secondary and tertiary. The primary tinder, which is the driest and finest available is the most desirable to make initial contact with the coal. The secondary tinder, which is slightly coarser helps to insulate the former. Lastly, the tertiary tinder may be used to hold it all together and to keep the coal from escaping the confines of the tinder bundle. The quality of the available tinder will dictate what combination of the aforementioned categories you will have to use.

After placing the coal inside, hold the tinder bundle as you would a sandwich, arms near full extension, slightly higher than your eyes. Too much pressure from your fingers will crush the coal. Too little pressure will not allow the coal to make the contact necessary to transfer the heat into the tinder. The wind should be at your back while coaxing fire from a coal. The prevailing wind will assist you in your efforts and carry the smoke away from your eyes.

To feed the coal, purse your lips as if drinking through a straw. Then push the air from your mouth in a strong, steady and silent fashion. Moments before the tinder gives birth to the flame, you will notice the smoke thickening. Be ready. Your fire lay should be built beforehand to receive the new flame.

Material Selection

Great care should be taken when choosing the materials for your fire. Obviously, it must be dry. Standing dead wood is more desirable than material lying on the ground. The initial fire lay should be configured so that a cavity exists in which you will place the flaming tinder.

In the early stages of a fire, it is best to begin with the pieces of wood roughly the thickness of matchsticks. The next layer should consist of pencil-size sticks. These smaller pieces will catch more quickly than larger ones; gather plenty of them. The rule of thumb is, gather twice as much firewood as you think you'll need. Then double it. The last thing you want is to be stumbling around in the dark looking for fuel for your fire.

7 - Security

We have an illusion of security; we don't have security.
—Isaac Yeffet

T HE INSTABILITY IN OUR NATION and indeed globally is increasing. It seems as though wedges have been driven into every social fault line imaginable. Our nation is divided, and we are witnessing a severe lack of civility. We the people? There isn't a "we" mentality anymore, nor has there been for a long time. Civil discourse is no longer practiced. Economically, we are walking the razor's edge. The geopolitical situation is only a breath away from yet another world war. It's not a matter of if, but when the first domino comes tumbling down.

There is no question our security situation will continue to deteriorate. Human history is filled with one example after another. It's happening again. All empires have a shelf life; the American Empire is disintegrating quickly. It should be glaringly obvious to all at this point of the possibility of such dangerous times. Even a cursory glance at the evening news will provide all the evidence you need. Law enforcement personnel have been impotent to stop the madness. Either that, or their administrations have been complicit. Either way, armed citizens will be the decisive factor.

When tensions rise, people become even more dangerous and unpredictable than they normally are. Cities have ground to a standstill in the face of such actions.

America is only one court decision away from gruesome violence. As I write this, the 2020 election looms on the horizon. Tensions are high at home and internationally. We'll see what happens.

Security efforts of this magnitude require numbers; you cannot do this alone! If you haven't already taken measures to build a security team, doing so should be a high priority. It seems time is not on our side; get busy.

This chapter will not satisfy all of the information and requirements essential to your security planning. Our purpose is to cause you to think about your situation and take action. This action should largely be in the form of reality-based training from a competent instructor. Additionally, we wish to present a general overview of skills, both for the individual and the group that must be learned if you are to be successful.

Personal Security

At any moment, you may find yourself in the wrong place at the wrong time, tangled up with the wrong people. What follows are some essential nuts and bolts for your survival machine.

- Situational Awareness
- Avoidance
- Reaction Gap
- De-escalation
- Unarmed Combatives
- Edged Weapons
- Impact Weapons
- Firearms
- Medical Considerations

Situational Awareness

The three pillars of a successful attack are:

- The Element of Surprise
- Speed
- Violence of Action

These pillars are well known and practiced by both law enforcement and military personnel. No fight was ever won by defense. Only a violent attack will yield victory. Conflict is not settled by using a shield; only the sword can settle the matter. Violence isn't always the answer. However, when violence is required, it is the ONLY answer.

You must strive to utilize these three pillars while denying their use by your adversary.

These days, folks spend a lot time looking down instead of paying attention to their surroundings. We tend to focus on our electronic devices rather than what is happening around us.

Humans really do possess an instinct that can sense danger. Listen to it. If a person, place or situation makes your skin crawl, you should create distance at a rapid pace. Don't question it, act.

Situational awareness takes practice. Become a watcher of people. What types of shoes are they wearing and why? What does their watch tell you about them? What stickers are on the vehicle? What are they looking at? Why are they looking at it? Do they fit the baseline of the local area and activities? If not, why not? Avoid staring or excessive eye contact, as this can have negative results. It's entirely possible to watch someone without being obvious about the fact you are watching.

Adopt a mentality of constantly war-gaming scenarios. What if someone starts shooting? Where are the exits? What could I use for cover? If for some reason I find myself unarmed, where could I obtain a weapon? I'm pretty sure every kitchen has at least one knife in it; commercial kitchens have really big ones with comfortable grips. What about that fire extinguisher on the wall? Just pay attention and listen to your gut.

If it's 90 degrees on the street and a dude approaches you in a hoody with the hood deployed and you can't see one or both of his hands, there's a good chance that he's up to no good, so avoid him if you can. If he attacks, you should already be expecting it and have made preparations to handle the situation.

Avoidance

If you're hanging out in a sketchy bar parking lot at three AM after the bar has closed, you may be creating your own tragedy. Endeavor to avoid people, places and activities that are questionable. Just because you can, doesn't mean you should.

During the course of your average day, despite your best efforts, questionable and sketchy may find you. In such a case, you should leave quickly, as soon as your radar goes off.

Note: Ladies in some cultures tend to be more submissive or less assertive than in other cultures. If you find yourself in a situation where you feel threatened, it is perfectly appropriate to raise hell, look a dude square in the eyes, issue verbal commands (you are TELLING, not asking) such as, STOP! BACK UP! NOW! While placing your hand on a weapon and preparing to kill the bastard if he doesn't listen.

The scumbags in society aren't usually looking for a fight, especially if there is a likelihood they will be injured. They are looking for a victim. Don't act like one! Don't be one! Set your mind to that and carry yourself accordingly. They will probably choose someone else.

Never allow yourself to be taken to a secondary crime scene. Example: If the bastard is trying to drag you into a van in the Walmart parking lot, fight to the death right there. It doesn't matter if he has a gun or a knife—it must end where it began. Bad guys really want to avoid making a scene. Your chances of survival are greatly diminished when you are taken to a secondary location. You can defeat him. His eyes and testicles are sensitive no matter how big he is or how much he can bench press.

On many occasions, I have seen one or more persons approaching and felt as though I should avoid them. Actions such as crossing the street or making a quick change of direction can go a long way toward keeping you out of trouble.

Reaction Gap

Some of us were doing this long before it was a government mandate, think tactical social distancing (TSD). Whenever possible, you should maintain a reaction gap between yourself and others. A reaction gap is the minimum amount of space you will allow someone to encroach; that gives you the time and space needed to react to a threat. Think of it as personal space or your bubble. It's better to be thought of as a little unfriendly than to allow someone to get so close that they can injure you before you can react. It is far easier to stay out of a chokehold than to get out of one.

De-Escalation

Avoid arguments and power struggles at all costs. At times, in spite of our best efforts, we may find ourselves in a confrontation with someone who is angry, unreasonable or mentally ill. It may not be possible to walk away immediately, and some exchange of words or communication may be necessary.

If the other party is angry, for some wrong, be it real or imagined, avoid escalating the situation by your words and actions. A smile and an apology may cool things off. Validation of the other person's feelings can also help bring a situation down to a manageable level where violence can be avoided. I know it sounds like psychobabble, but people really just want to know they have been heard and understood even if they know they are wrong.

Example Scenario:

Them: *What the hell man?*

You: *Oh, sorry I bumped into you*

Them: *Hey asshole, you made me spill my coffee. This is a new shirt!*

You: *I understand that you're angry, you know, I probably would be too. Again, very sorry, didn't see you there, honest mistake, my bad. Here's $20 for another coffee and the cleaning bill. Gotta run, my brother's outside waiting for me.*

Exit and make distance rapidly even if you didn't get your coffee. There's another coffee shop down the street. This is not the time to argue over who is right or wrong. The situation isn't that severe, and you don't know what is happening in that guy's life. He may be fresh out of prison and on the way to a job interview. The twenty spot you gave him will be much cheaper than the medical and legal expenses should you escalate the situation. In addition, the people observing this confrontation will later testify to the fact that you were not the aggressor should things turn violent and you were forced to defend yourself.

Unarmed Combatives

You did everything right. You maintained awareness of your surroundings; you crossed the street when you noticed the two roguish gentlemen lurking in the shadows. Then, they crossed the street and started walking faster, then faster. "Hey, man, what are you looking at?" the first man says as he closes with you. Before you can utter a single word, his partner has disappeared behind some parked cars and reappears on your back choking the life out of you as you both fall to the concrete. His accomplice proceeds to kick you in the ribs repeatedly while the other continues the choking process. People are standing around, but no one seems willing to intervene on your behalf. In fact, several of them are filming the incident with their cellphones while some of the bystanders cheer them on.

You have a concealed handgun, but is this the time to draw it? Both of your hands are clawing at the man's arm, fighting for a breath of air, the chokehold is working. Things are starting to go dark.

Do you have the skills to survive this situation? You won't find them in this book or any other book. Hands-on, reality-based training with non-compliant training partners is the *only* way to build proficiency in unarmed combatives.

Just because you have a gun doesn't mean it's always the answer. In many situations, it is more appropriate to strike, escape from a hold, create space then access your weapon. You always have your body parts with you, learn to weaponize them! If your gun goes skittering across the parking lot, you still need to finish the fight.

Mean, nasty violence can only be overcome by meaner, nastier violence. You must develop the mindset of being a savage, ruthless, unforgiving individual that will literally rip out the eyeballs of your opponent and urinate in the remaining voids. The one that lands the first decisive blow and maintains the operational momentum usually wins. Your mindset is more powerful than you can possibly imagine. Develop it now.

Edged Weapons

The knife is our oldest and most basic tool. It's also a formidable weapon. It won't jam, misfire or run out of ammunition. No batteries are required; it's a beautiful thing.

I have a pretty extensive martial arts background. Many books have been written on knife fighting and many martial arts systems are devoted to the use of knives. I don't wish to over-complicate the matter, so I will simply direct you to a small excerpt from The Reluctant Partisan, Volume One by John Mosby. In this masterpiece, Mr. Mosby states the following:

"Knife fighting is killing the other guy, using your knife. There's no fighting to it. Using a knife to kill is retard-simple: put the pointy end in the soft spots. Repeat as necessary. It really is that simple. Stab the f***er in the eye, throat, sides of the neck, stomach, groin, or lower back, and keep stabbing him, repeatedly, as fast as you can. He will go down, and he will bleed out." Thus endeth the quote.

When we take Mr. Mosby's real-world advice and couple it with an understanding of surprise, speed and violence of action, the three pillars previously listed, a real-world version of knife usage comes into view. It ain't pretty, but it is effective.

Impact weapons

Any item that makes our sphere of influence longer or stronger can be considered a weapon. A weapon is simply a tool that allows us to project violence over distance. The greater the distance, the better the weapon. In areas where the carry of firearms or knives is not possible, impact weapons may have to suffice. A flashlight with a strike bezel and pocket clip is a fine weapon. A wooden cane may be carried along with a cover story as to why. Many urban cyclists carry a bike lock on a chain around their waist, these have proven fearsome weapons in a melee. A common writing pen can be violently gripped and used in a stabbing and ripping action, targeting the soft spots previously discussed.

A nice skull crusher can be improvised by placing a padlock or similar hefty object into a sock or bandanna. Tie strong knots to secure the item, then use the remaining portion as a handle. This can be carried in a pocket or in the waistband with the handle portion exposed or concealed for rapid deployment. I have personally witnessed such items being used and I can attest to their effectiveness.

Firearms

The main advantage afforded by firearms is the ability to project force and influence over distance. Additionally, they enable the user to overcome disadvantages such as multiple attackers or a disparity of force. America is a well-armed nation. The problem I see is that the vast majority of gun owners have all the stuff but very little actual skill that would be of service to them in a life and death struggle. Marksmanship is one thing. OK, so you can hit a target. Awesome. Can you clear that malfunction with one hand because your other arm has been injured (or otherwise occupied defending yourself) and is no longer functioning? You do carry a tourniquet with you at all times, right? Can you do all that without looking? It might be dark.

Have you ever been shot at? No? Then I HIGHLY recommend forceon-force training. You will find the experience more rewarding than shooting paper targets. Force-on-force training is one of the best tools available to prepare you for a real gunfight.

Recommended training: The Fight, Tactical Response, Camden TN Get. Some. Training. NOW! Don't give me this static about, "Oh, but it's expensive." What is your life worth? The lives of your family members may depend on YOU! Do you want to be a C student or an A+ student? Get some training. No one is coming to save you! Law enforcement officers are called first responders for a reason; they respond AFTER the damage has been done.

Medical Considerations

Interpersonal violence is a dynamic thing. After the action, it is common that one or more parties involved have sustained some type of injury. At a minimum, every member of your family should have a working knowledge of CPR and first aid. The use of tourniquets and pressure dressings should be mastered. Books are fine for use as reference material. Again, there is no substitute for reality-based hands-on training.

Securing the Homestead

From a security standpoint, the modern American home is a joke. Think about it for a second, we have doors made of, wait for it…glass. The walls of most modern homes consist of nothing more than thin vinyl siding, Styrofoam, plywood and drywall. These materials *will not* stop bullets. These materials are also quite flammable. Our homes seem as if they were built to burn. The location of the typical modern dwelling is also laughable. Our homes are often situated close to and visible from a road, usually within pistol range.

Without electricity, water resupply isn't an option for the vast majority of today's homes. Additionally, the land upon which these homes are situated lacks the means to produce food in the long term. An honest appraisal of 98% of American homes, from a survival and security perspective would rightly send the owner into a frenzied search for a real estate agent. While relocation isn't an option for everyone, I submit that living in an area with high population density is a recipe for death and disaster.

In my travels abroad, I have seen many houses consisting of glass doors and windows. The difference being the glass is covered with steel bars; oftentimes accompanied by a small courtyard consisting of walls, razor wire and more steel bars. These walls were built of more robust material such as brick, block, concrete and stone. This is typical in the more population-dense areas of Africa, Central and South America and the Caribbean. To gain physical entry, one must penetrate two hardened rings of security. This denies the intruder the element of surprise and buys time for the occupants to mount a defense.

As you venture into the more rural areas, the structures tend to be less fortress like, such as wood frame and grass thatch huts. The conclusion: more people equal more problems. There is generally a universal difference between urban dwellers and country folk, regardless of the nation in which they reside.

One need only conduct a short study of the localized disasters such as Hurricane Katrina or any number of riots that have occurred in recent years to gain some perspective on the security issue. The unrest usually takes place in a population-dense area. I don't recall seeing farmers in rural areas smashing store windows and burning things down. I have noticed a pattern of looting and violence in urban areas though.

In light of these facts, we can rightly conclude that the first step to good security is a good location.

Note: When selecting a location, your first course of action should be to conduct a thorough study of the area. You should consider such factors as lines of drift (more on that later), proximity to chemical factories, military bases and power plants to name a few.

Things to Consider

- A *reliable* water source
- Avoid lines of drift
- Housing not visible from the road
- Housing on secondary or tertiary road
- Land suitable for food production
- Adequate storage for provisions
- Security team/community
- A physical barrier or obstacles between you and the bad guys

This list is by no means all-inclusive, but it will give you a good start.

Let's examine each item in more detail.

A Reliable Water Source

The key word here is reliable. If the power grid is down, how will you get water? Without water you will be forced to physically relocate. You will go to where there is water, or you will die. For this reason, my first question is always, "Where's the water?" For example, my location has a private well. The problem is when the electricity is out, the pump doesn't work. To remedy this, a hand pump was installed. There is also a natural water source about seventy yards from the house as a back-up. Without water there is no security because dehydrated, dead people cannot fight.

Avoid Lines of Drift

Wikipedia defines natural lines of drift as: "Those paths across terrain that are the most likely to be used when going from one place to another. These paths are paths of least resistance: those that offer the greatest ease while taking into account obstacles (e.g. rivers, cliffs, dense unbroken woodland, etc.) and modes of transit (e.g. pedestrian, automobile, horses). Common endpoints or fixed endpoints may include water sources, food sources and obstacle passages such as fords or bridges.

Local paths may be derived from game trails or from artificial paths created by utility lines or political boundaries. Property ownership and land use may also be factors in determining local variations.

Improved paths may also be partially defined by the logistics necessary to build roads or railways.

If you have a railway, interstate, highway or utility lines running through, near or within walking distance of where you sleep, now would be a good time to give the realtor a ring! Remember, people equal problems and lines of drift will funnel people right to your doorstep if your location is poorly chosen.

Housing Area Not Visible from Roads

The old saying, "Out of sight, out of mind," is as true today as it ever was. People usually like to have a look at the target before they attack. Often, criminals will go through a planning phase before launching a home invasion or other action. This is not always true though, as some actions are spontaneous, targets of opportunity.

The amount of information that can be gleaned by driving, walking or jogging past a house cannot be underestimated.

Bad guy: "Oh, I see two vehicles so probably two adults live there (most people over eighteen years of age have their own car). Oh look, an NRA and Glock bumper sticker. They are probably armed. We should surprise them and bring a few extra guys for this one. We could use more guns. I bet they have a few. Ahhh, a stick figure family on the back of Mom's minivan. They have three kids, one boy plays soccer, the other practices karate and the girl is a cheerleader. I don't see any sign of guard dogs. The lighting sucks here at night; that's good for us. No indications of an alarm system, but I don't think it matters the power has been out for four days since the storm and I haven't seen any cops. There is no gate or fence, so we will be able to back the van right up to the front door. That door ain't shit. We'll be in quickly. Actually, I'm thinking of sending a couple of guys around back so we can come in both doors at the same time. That's a nice house, nice cars. I'll bet they have a lot of nice stuff. I wonder how old that cheerleader is?"

Get the picture? If moving is not an option for you, I would urge you to look at your home from the outside with evil intent. Have your buddy who has military or law enforcement experience do the same. Then take the feedback you receive and make adjustments. Above all, scrape those damned stickers off your car and stop giving the bad guys information! Do what you can to harden your home.

A final thought, distance is your friend when it comes to security. The further away your home is from the public road, the more time you will have to react to people as they cross the line from public to private property. Pressure + distance = tactics.

Housing on a Secondary or Tertiary Road

This topic ties into the subject of lines of drift, which was previously discussed, only the focus is more specific concerning roads or what may be referred to as high-speed avenues of approach.

For obvious reasons, a house immediately adjacent to a main road is at a distinct disadvantage where security is concerned. I think we all understand the concept of a main, or primary road. Let us define a secondary road as one that turns away from the main road, leading off in another direction, or to a given area that is more loosely populated. A tertiary road, for our purposes, will turn off from the secondary road and lead to essentially nowhere of particular interest. In other words, people traveling in that area mean to come there or they are lost. Generally speaking, there is considerably little traffic on tertiary roads. Tertiary roads are also much less likely to see heavy traffic in case of mass human movement through an area.

Land Suitable for Food Production

Again, without adequate food production, no security is possible. Your food storage will eventually be depleted. Then what? Choose a location that lends itself to long term food sustainability. Go ahead and plant blueberries, apple orchards or whatever is appropriate for your locale. Build raised beds, prepare the ground and be sure to have the required tools and the heirloom seeds to continue into the future. Get those projects done now while times are good. Believe it or not, these ARE the good ole days.

You simply cannot store enough food. At some point, no matter how much you have stored, it will run out. In a short-term emergency, your food stores can see you through. But in a long duration event, or like what we foresee, a foundational shift in our society that could last a decade or better, you WILL have to be able to produce your own food.

Adequate Storage for Provisions

Good security is an around-the-clock endeavor. Water, food, adequate clothing and equipment are directly linked to security. If you are starving, you will not be focused on security, you will be focused on finding something to eat. A retreat location should be stocked with enough provisions to ensure adequate caloric intake, hydration and equipment. It is my opinion that a food supply calculated to last at least a year is minimal. This, along with clothing, bedding and other supplies will require enough physical space to store it all.

Security Team/Community

The romantic notion of the lone survivor battling the forces of evil, while simultaneously meeting all of the requirements essential to sustain a healthy life is utter steaming, dripping, bullshit. Mom and pop on the mountain top guarding their pile of beans with a shotgun ain't gonna secure much! They will likely die in place upon first contact with an aggressing force.

Security is definitely a game of numbers. You must sleep at some point. One person can only look in one direction. What's happening around back while you're watching the front? Who's on duty while you cook a meal, chop wood or carry water?

Even four or six people will stand a better chance in a fight than two, but they must have skills! They must be trained! Do you see a recurring theme here? Training, training, training.....

When would you prefer to be aware of an enemy presence? As they are kicking in your door, at your mailbox, or a mile down the road?

The obvious answer would be as far away as possible. How will you accomplish this? You DO have a hidden observation post down the road manned by two dudes with rifles and radios, right? Given this information, what will you do about the situation? "The intruders are a mile away, two vehicles, four men per vehicle, visibly armed. Smoke can be seen in the distance as the neighbor's house burns to the ground. Oh no! That's Laura, the neighbor's daughter hog-tied in the back of the truck..."

Sounds farfetched? You don't think it can happen here? It is happening somewhere, right now as you read this! Human trafficking is alive and well globally, and yes, even here in America. During the collapse, these types of behaviors will intensify. I digress. So, back to you on the homestead, what will you do?

Can your team of daring survivors scramble to conduct a hasty ambush? Can you shoot straight enough, while being shot at, to stop all the bad guys and not put a bullet through Laura? Can you treat the wounded afterwards? Bullets go both ways; you're not shooting paper targets anymore. Remember, the bad guy gets a vote as well. Somebody is bound to get hurt. Expect it.

Look! Now the house is on fire! A couple of vehicles pulled up around back while you were down the road. They took all your stuff and torched the house. Where's Bobby? Dead of a heart attack because he wasn't physically ready to run down the street and endure the stress of a gunfight. Preparation matters. Fitness matters. Training matters.

You've got a grave to dig. Then what? Where will your family sleep tonight? You do have supplies in multiple locations, right? You do have an alternate location or mutual assistance agreement I would hope.

This is not meant to scare or overwhelm you. It is the purpose of the authors to cause you to think, plan and prepare. You cannot do this alone. Your security team should have a working knowledge of the following, at a bare minimum. This list is by no means the end-all, be-all. Our purpose is to simply shed some light on the tasks that lie before you. The following items are in no particular order and represent both individual and collective (group) skills. Using the previous section on personal security as a foundation, you should additionally seek to attain proficiency in:

- Physical fitness
- Unarmed Combatives
- Pistol operation (marksmanship, malfunctions, cleaning, repair, etc.)
- Rifle operation (marksmanship, malfunctions, cleaning, repair, etc.)
- First aid/CPR
- Advanced medical training
- Individual movement techniques
- Use of cover/concealment
- Principles of camouflage
- Assembly of load-bearing equipment (what to carry and why)
- Assembly of a backpack to be used while in the field, patrolling, etc.
- Land navigation (map and compass)
- Wilderness survival
- Water crossing techniques
- Hide site construction/observation post
- Security patrolling on foot
- Security patrolling in vehicles

- Communications
- Small unit tactics
- Room clearing

This list is by no means complete but I think it conveys the point that there is much to learn. Each of the previous bullet points is a detailed course of study in itself with many nuances. I have read about them and I have done them all. The real learning is in the doing.

I do not wish to reinvent a wheel that already exists, so I will simply direct you to some masterful works that have already been written. (See appendix).

Has it Been Pressure Tested?

I carry a special confidence. Why? I've been pressure tested. I don't think, I know that I can get the job done. I have intentionally put myself in situations that will crush a person, tool or tactic if they can't perform when it really counts. I will never place my trust in anything or anyone that hasn't been pressure tested. Please don't mistake this as being cocky or overconfident. It's actually quite the opposite. Everyone and everything have limits. The difference lies in the fact that I know exactly where my breaking points are. I know my limits and that of my equipment because I try to break everything. Then I ask myself the question, why did it break?

Every piece of equipment that I have chosen to carry is the result of pressure testing. If I place impossible demands on a piece of kit and it doesn't fail, I *know* I can bet my life on it.

There are very few people that I know who can be trusted. They all have one thing in common. They have been pressure tested. They have proven that they will perform when all others have failed or produced excuses as to why they can't. People are a double-edged sword. They are arguably your greatest asset. At the same time, people are usually the source of trouble. People don't always say what they really mean, but they say and do things designed to get what they want. It's easy to figure people out, just sit back and watch. If you are doing all the giving in the relationship, cut them lose. If they constantly produce excuses as to why they can't learn or train, let them go. There is no place for dead weight. The maximum effective range of an excuse is exactly zero.

I have been pressure tested. My equipment has been pressure tested. My relationships (the ones that matter) have been pressure tested. There are precious few people that I actually fully trust. They are my inner circle; they have been pressure tested.

There is a reoccurring theme in the prepper community. People are giving themselves and their fellows more credit than they deserve. They don't know what they don't know because they haven't been pressure tested. I have actually had people tell me that this weekend wouldn't be a good time to train because it's too, (insert excuse here) cold, hot, wet, whatever. If you are only willing to practice and train in fair weather, how will you ever learn to perform in a snowstorm, when you're sick, injured, hungry and sleep deprived. The answer is you will never know. The more hideous the weather, the better the training.

You will never grow inside your comfort zone. You must suffer if you really want to grow as a person. Adversity builds character and inner strength. Every lesson that I have ever learned, that was worth learning, involved pain in one form or another. Adversity and pain are the chisels that chip away the unnecessary parts of you, leaving a beautiful statue when the work is finished. Suffering has its place and nothing bonds people more surely than mutual suffering.

I would encourage you to look at everything and everyone in your life and ask the question, has it been pressure tested? If it hasn't, then you do not know what it truly is or what it is capable of. If your *friend* keeps handing out excuses as to why he can't show up, he won't show up. If people can't do it now when the doing is easy, cut them lose.

Knowing weakness and failure points will give you a realistic picture of your actual capabilities. Thus, you will make better decisions because you are basing those decisions on what you *really know*. Assumption is a dangerous tactic. Know yourself. Know your people. Know your gear. Pressure test them. Adjustments will be much more difficult to make on game day. And the lessons will come at a much higher price.

Physical Barriers/Obstacles

It's much more difficult for unsavory bipeds to attack by surprise if they must first negotiate an obstacle or barrier. If a truck crashes through the gate at the end of your driveway, it's a safe bet that they are not census takers paying a visit. It would be even better if you built your gate so that it couldn't be crashed through; then they must come at you on foot.

The first step to security is to define the area you wish to secure. This is called a perimeter. The perimeter is your line in the sand, so to speak. You're saying to the bad guys, "Ye shall not pass further". A perimeter fence is a good idea because they must come under, through or over it to have at you. Just be sure that the barriers and obstacles you construct can't be used as cover for the enemy to hide behind and shoot at you. That's why I prefer wire. Consider this...

- Detect
- Deter
- Delay
- Defend

A good perimeter fence, tangle foot wire, or both, will deter and delay entry or attack. The detect and defend requirement must be satisfied by a hard-hearted human with a rifle who is watching the wire from a concealed position. Without this thinking human element, they will simply come back with the necessary tools and cut through the wire. There are many options for obstacles, barriers and barricades. Do the research and implement the plan that is appropriate for your situation.

Night Vision Equipment (NODS)

Night vision equipment is the single most useful piece of technology that will give you a distinct advantage over those that don't have it.

A good portion of the twenty-four-hour cycle is occupied by a no-light or low-light environment. It is during this time that the wooly boogers come out to play. Possessing the ability to direct accurate small arms fire on them is a real game changer. There are limitations to technology though.

If the camouflage, movement and concealment of the bad guys is on point, you still may not see them. If you wouldn't be able to see them in daylight, you won't see them with night vision either. Thermal imaging may pick up where the night vision leaves off. Thermal imaging also has limitations. Thermal imaging will not enable you to see through glass or extremely dense vegetation. The best situation would be to have both, but they are quite expensive.

Batteries are the Achilles heel of modern technology so be sure to plan for that.

The PVS-14 is a game-changer. Having one allows you to own the night.

In conjunction with quality night vision, the MAWL allows you to accurately employ your rifle in the dark. This is a huge advantage.

The Rifle

The rifle, in competent hands, is the most useful tool to guarantee your safety, security and liberty. For the purpose of self-preservation, the rifle should be semi-automatic, of a commonly available caliber with standard capacity magazines, holding twenty to thirty rounds, depending on the type chosen. The owner of such an implement must train diligently in its safe, lawful usage.

During times of chaos, the rifle will enable a 120 pound, 60-year-old woman to say no to a group of miscreants of questionable virtue and low breeding approaching her home and enable her to have the teeth to enforce her verbal assertions. She can say no at a distance and avoid battling the criminals on their terms in a wrestling match.

There is much debate these days concerning such weapons. It's all pretty clear to me. A study of history easily reveals what happens without them. We made alcohol illegal. How did that work out? The war on drugs has been raging for quite some time, yet I will wager

A properly configured rifle and web gear (LBE) to support that rifle are a must. Either is useless without the other.

that drugs can be found at your local high school. Prohibiting a thing doesn't make it disappear. Bad people will always find the tools they need to do bad things.

I have traveled extensively outside the United States. In every case, even in countries where firearms were forbidden or severely restricted by law, the bad guys always had them and used them plenty.

No rifle is complete without a practical set of load bearing equipment (LBE). A rifle-toting individual without the ability to carry additional magazines, medical gear and other essential equipment would be the equivalent of having a car with no tires; you won't go very far. A good LBE setup will support the rifle and the operator. LBE is of the utmost importance. Additionally, a quality sling is an absolute must. You may need both hands to perform a given task and the sling will enable you to keep your rifle on your body.

The rifle is a cumbersome thing. It's also impractical and socially unacceptable to roll through the grocery store with one slung across your back. For those days when your neighborhood isn't on fire, something more discreet is required. Let's consider the pistol.

The Pistol

In everyday life, while things are "normal' (whatever that means; a setting on your dryer according to some), the modern pistol is the most practical tool for self-preservation. Such a thing can be discreetly carried on one's person and ready for use. As with everything in this book, you must receive proper training and practice regularly to be effective in the real world.

I do not wish to enter the endless debate over which model or caliber is best. However, I do speak with the Almighty on a regular basis and He has assured me that if He needed a pistol, it would be a Glock chambered in nine-millimeter. Amen.

Human history, indeed, modern American history, is filled with examples of people behaving savagely. Such occurrences have lasted for days and weeks before any sense of normalcy has been reestablished.

One could argue that the aftermath of the hurricanes in Puerto Rico have left the island unstable as much as a year after landfall. Many people, including a significant portion of the police force are packing up and coming stateside. My friends who are still there tell me that crime is steadily worsening.

In my opinion, every defensive pistol should have a light. An RMR is a valuable addition, though it takes some training to get used to it.

Then there are the examples of Greece, Argentina and Venezuela, to name only a few. Can it happen here? You bet! It will happen here, and it *has* happened here before. It will happen again. Only this time, I fear the bar will be raised to new levels.

Operational Security/ Privacy Considerations

What follows are a few thoughts on privacy and operational security considerations for freedom-loving individuals in these precarious times. I attended a firearms class one day. At the end of the class, one of the attendees, whom I've never met, said the following "Ya'll wanna take a group picture while we've still got all our gear on?" Without hesitation, I said, "Nope! That's how the NSA finds you, bro." I was kind of joking, kind of not. That got me thinking…

How much information do we put out there? I would wager that all class participants brought a cell phone with them that day. Some may say, "Well, we're not doing anything wrong or illegal." That's not really the point. Another may say, "We're just exercising our rights. I'm totally legal. I filled out papers for my gun at the store when I bought it and I've got my permit." Exactly.

Let's just look at the paperwork and the permit for a minute. The paperwork you filled out is basically "gun registration." The permit you obtained turned your precious "right" into a privilege. If you actually had that "right," you would have no need to pay money to a government entity to issue you a card (permission) to exercise that "right", which should also never expire as true rights have no expiration date.

Furthermore, that photo and those fingerprints you submitted will most assuredly be placed in a database containing those biometrics, along with mountains of other data that you have willingly surrendered. Land of the free! But is it though? People intent on criminal mischief do not jump through these hoops, but that's ok. This tracking and data storage isn't for them anyway. It's targeting you, me and anyone who believes as we do.

Just think about it. By obtaining a permit to exercise what we believe to be a "God-given right", that "shall not be infringed", you are actually saying the following:

1. I have at least one weapon and the inclination to use it.

2. You really don't believe any of that "from my cold dead hands" rubbish that you post on Facebook and they know it. I'm not trying to offend anyone—just being a realist.

3. Now that they have your faces, fingerprints, addresses, family trees, known contacts and everywhere you've traveled over the past few years, they should have no problem finding which door to kick down when they deem you a "threat".

4. Now, we are not only willingly giving, but paying for the privilege, to provide .Gov with our DNA! Imagine if Hitler had had access to that kind of information.

Let's look at a few other things:

Your phone. The amount of data gathered from the average person's phone is mind boggling; everywhere you have traveled, the duration of your stay, and who was around you. "Hmmm. You guys look like a terror cell to me."

Every website you visit, every video you watch and every online purchase you have made has not gone unnoticed. Furthermore, that information is stored indefinitely and can be swept into a nice, neat little pile at any given time in the future to scrutinize you and develop an eerily accurate profile of who you really are and what you are likely to do given a certain stimulus. *Social media.* I think it's obvious that a government think tank filled with psychologists and sociologists would have lots of material to work with if given our social media data. This material really adds up over time.

In fact, they probably know us better than we know ourselves!

I don't know much, but I do know this. I am less free than my father, he was less free than my grandfather who was less free than my great grandfather. What level of freedom, if any, will our children inherit from us? Are we nothing more than free-range citizens on a government tax farm?

Our forebearers would never have tolerated what passes as freedom today, but we are not them, obviously.

> *"If ye love wealth better than liberty, the tranquility of servitude better than the animating contest of freedom, go home from us in peace. We ask not your counsels or arms. Crouch down and lick the hands which feed you. May your chains set lightly upon you, and may posterity forget that ye were our countrymen."*
> —Samuel Adams

Before sharing personal information, such as, *I have five years of food stored in the basement*, ask yourself, does this person need to know this? The old adage, loose lips sink ships is just as relevant today and possibly more so than it was in the forties.

8 - Chow Time

A hungry man is not a free man.
—Adlai E. Stevenson

I F HUMANS ARE TO CONTINUE life on the planet, we must return to the land. We must once again establish an intimate connection with our food and pluck it from the earth with our very own hands. Many fancy themselves as self-reliant; close examination will likely prove their belief false.

"Oh, I'm a good hunter; I'll feed my family venison and we'll be fine." Indeed, you may. However, self-reliant is an inaccurate label to hang on it. Let's examine the average hunt. Our great hunter grabs a $700 rifle with $400 (or more) scope. He then hops into his pickup truck that he likely makes monthly payments to keep, valued at tens of thousands. In the bed of the truck, we find a treestand, another $300, if you're hunting in the east. It's also not uncommon for a trailer, $2000 more, with an ATV, purchased on sale for the bargain price of $10,000, to be attached to such a chariot. Both the truck and the ATV are dependent on petrol.

Our hunter arrives on location clad in specialized clothing and footwear that he didn't make. He probably doesn't know the person that did make them. Many times, our hunter will return empty-handed. But, let's just assume he was successful. He dresses the deer and uses the ATV to transport his harvest back to the truck. Then he drives home. He then cuts up the kill, or more likely takes it to a processor and is most likely dependent on electricity to preserve it for later use.

A well-stocked pantry.

Our hunter did not craft a single piece of clothing or equipment with his own hands. Nor did he source a single piece of it from nature. Additionally, he is 100% dependent on the petrol and power grid. How is this self-reliance? When the bad thing happens, hunting will look much different than it does now. You will walk, not drive. You will carry and drag your equipment and quarry, should you be lucky. Your personal security will be foremost in your mind. The competition will be fierce. Preserving your kill will probably be done by means of smoke.

Not only is this not self-reliant, it's also not even sustainable. Just consider the logistics chain it took to get all that together. The hundreds of people involved in the mining, manufacturing and distribution of these goods, all for a single hunt! And please, do not get us wrong. We are not anti-hunting, quite the opposite. The point here is to get you to think about what it takes to enjoy this hobby, for that's all it is if we are truly honest with ourselves. You may be a hunter, but Davey Crockett you ain't!

The population density in America, coupled with the fact that we are extremely well-armed, assures that most game will become nearly extinct in a relatively short period of time. The woods will be teeming with very well-armed, very desperate people. To put this in perspective, in the early 1900s, deer populations in the US were at an all-time low. In many areas, they were nearly extirpated from the land, almost extinct. It was so severe in many states that the mere sighting of a whitetail deer was noteworthy. We only have wild game in this country because we have chosen to do so. For context, the US population in 1900 was 76,212,168. We are now nearly four times that number. Game will vanish from the land, consumed like a wildfire faster than you can imagine.

"Well, I have a year's worth of food put away; we'll be fine." That's awesome. I applaud your efforts. Until recent history, many peoples maintained food stores to see them through the winter. We should all gain and maintain deep reserves of food. Many foods can be stored indefinitely, and technology has enabled us to obtain packaged foods that will likely keep for decades. What happens when your reserves have been exhausted? The answer, you must be able to produce, preserve, and secure your own food. "Ah, we grow a garden every year and my wife cans it up; we'll survive." That's great. Do you grow and preserve this garden with no dependence on petrol, electricity, fertilizer or pesticide? Can you successfully bring your crops to fruition without the tractor and tiller? Do you have the means and manpower to secure it around the clock? You will not be the only person with an interest in your garden. Are you dependent on the purchase of seed each year or do you save your own?

I recommend a diversified approach for stomach insurance. We insure our homes, our vehicles and our health. Why not insure our ability to eat? Every family should begin by having a robust food storage plan. Opinions vary as to how much food you should store. I believe a year's supply to be the absolute minimum. More is always better. You will never have too much food; get busy.

The ability to hunt is good, but the ability to trap is so much better. Trapping allows you to accomplish other things while the traps work for you. Trapping is a game of numbers. Twenty traps set by one trapper will far outperform a tree stand occupied by one hunter. In addition to being skilled at trapping, hunting and fishing, it is essential that you learn to forage from the plant and insect kingdom.

Hunting and trapping excursions are some-times unsuccessful. Foraging on the other hand ensures the ability to obtain food anytime. The ultimate desired end state of the survivor is to procure food independent of the grid and supply chain. All of the aforementioned will have a cumulative effect, ensuring the survival of your family.

Food Storage

Purchasing more of what you already consume is a good place to start. I know some will bemoan the expense. I would simply ask, what's your life worth? Most of us can find the money within our budgets. Instead of yet another useless trip to the amusement park or the beach, put that money towards something tangible. I have friends that lost fortunes in the financial crisis of 2008. Had they put their money into tangible goods and paid down their debt, they would have fared better.

The next step is to store vast quantities of bulk foods such as wheat, beans, rice and oats. They can be found packaged in number ten cans that can be easily handled by the young and elderly, as opposed to fifty-pound bags For another option, using mylar bags and food grade buckets, you can package your own foods for the long haul.

According to Statista, the average Somali consumes 1,695 calories per day.

Average Caloric Content of one cup of the following:
Rice: 158
Oats: 234
Pinto Beans: 143
Garbanzo Beans: 729
Lentils: 230

Now, imagine your daily diet consisting of two cups of cooked oats in the morning. Your midday meal being a cup of garbanzo beans, a cup of lentils and two cups of rice and your evening meal being a cup of pinto beans and a cup and a half of rice. And you have to eat this every... single... day. To make this happen, you need to store the following.

Pounds of each
Rice: 165
Oats: 73
Pinto: 98
Garbanzo: 98
Lentils: 98

That's a total of 528 pounds of food for one person or 2,112 pounds, over a ton, for a family of four for one year.

And that's to eat like a Somali!

I would imagine you'd want to eat better than that!

Do you have that much food stored? In a collapse, you will burn more calories than you do now. Survival is hard work. Carrying water, gathering and processing fuel for cooking is a real calorie burner. Not to mention, providing security and tending to the daily needs of life. Keep these numbers in mind when friends and family say they'll, *just come to your house.*

I'm sure you would prefer to enjoy a more fulfilling diet, so let's take a look at the numbers for the good ole U.S. of A.

We Americans like to eat, a lot. Our diets contain way more calories than the average person needs considering the nature of the semi-sedentary lives we live. The modern world has removed a great deal of the *work* from our work. Depending on where you look, the average American consumes between 3,000-3,600 calories a day. At the upper end of that scale we are nearly two-thousand calories above our Somali counterparts.

The recommended daily caloric intake for the average female according to the USDA is 1,600-2,000. The average for men is 2,000-3,000. The British National Health Service differs a bit and gives us a little more perspective. They state women need 2,000 and men need 2,500. As you can see, they are both in the same range. It must be remembered that these numbers are for the *average* (whatever that means to these agencies) adult conducting nothing more than, *the requirements of independent living,* whatever that is.

In a crisis situation, those numbers will go up considerably. To get an idea of just how many calories a person will need when engaged in heavy physical labor, let's look at what the average hiker of the Appalachian Trail requires.

According to DietandFitness.com, the average athletic male, standing 5'11" and weighing in at 175 pounds (this is far below the *real* average) will consume 689 calories an hour hiking mountainous terrain carrying a 21 to 42-pound pack. While the average female (*stats were not given, you never ask a woman how much she weighs. Everyone knows that!*) will consume 591 calories during that same hour. So, if our average men and women are working 5.5 hours a day in heavy physical labor, we can see that the male will burn, 3789.5 calories and the female will burn, 3250.5 calories.

While you may be thinking that's no big deal, there's more to the story. We must also consider the basal metabolic rate (BMR). This is the number of calories the body burns if all you did was sit under a tree all day and not move. Just a like an engine, our bodies need fuel even at an idle. According to WebMD, the average male's BMR is 2,163 calories. So, to get to a total number of calories, we have to add the calories burned during the physical labor to the BMR for the daily total.

When we do, we see that number jumps to 5,952.5 calories a day! And that is just to maintain current bodyweight. Drop below that and you will begin to lose weight. It's estimated that 3,500 calories is equal to one pound of fat. So, if we are missing a thousand calories a day, we see that we'll lose one pound every three and half days.

It is important to keep these numbers in mind when we are planning our food storage. We took a look at several of the major long-term food storage companies' one-month supply for one person options to see how many calories they contained. Surprisingly, several of the best well-known companies didn't even give a total calorie count. The rest ranged from 1,854-2,000 calories a day, far below what we would actually burn.

It is also important to remember that most of these kits consisted of powdered *meals* in the form of soups, stews and oatmeal. Imagine eating such gruel for a month and think about how badly you would want a *real* meal. Something like a hamburger or a steak. Something with a hearty chew or a satisfying crunch when you took a bite.

Menu fatigue is a real thing. Being limited to a few options with little to no variety in taste or texture will be a real drain on morale. It could render eating into a dreaded chore entered into with no more enthusiasm that hauling water or chopping wood. And while it may not be practical for all to have a wide diverse variety of food, it is important to try and do so. Even one meal a week or every couple of days will give you something to look forward to. A reward such as this is a major psychological boost and that can be just as important as the calories and nutrients of the food itself.

A good diet should include a healthy balance of the following:

- Proteins
- Vitamins
- Minerals
- Carbohydrates
- Fats
- Salt

A *robust* food storage program is one of the most important things you can do for your family. *We cannot stress this enough!* Not only is it that important, food storage is also the easiest thing to do. This is where simply *buying* things really makes a difference. No one is coming to save you. Get busy.

Hunting

Hunting is what you do when you've done everything else. Sometimes while performing other tasks, the perfect shot will present itself. Have something with you to make that shot, always. Practice moving stealthily on the land. Pay attention to the prevailing wind direction. Use all your senses. Take measures to cover your scent. Learn all you can about the intended prey. Study them. Become them. You must learn to think as they do.

Tracking is an additional skill needed in the quiver of the hunter. Many a critter has been lost due to a deficiency in this skill. After you make your shot, sit quietly for several minutes. Listen, feel with all your senses. If you give chase immediately after the shot, you will only cause your beast to run farther due to your pressure.

Lastly, be careful with your thoughts, intention and eye contact. Animals can feel this. So can you. Have you ever had that feeling that something was watching you intently, then looking up, you confirm it to be true? I think we all have at one time or another. Become like a tree or a rock in your mind. I know it sounds esoteric, but there is definitely something to it. Trapping can go a long way towards keeping meat in the pot. Crafting trap triggers is a good way to pass the time and be productive during inclement weather. Most traps are basically a device that stores energy that is released by means of a trigger. I generally lean towards deadfalls, snares and gill nets to satisfy my salivation.

A good trap is like a good restaurant; it's all about location. Take care to disturb the environment as little as possible. Utilize logs, rocks and naturally occurring terrain to channel the critter to the trap. If the trap is near a burrow or on a game trail, the location itself may be enough for success. When possible, use bait. I recommend obtaining a book dedicated to the subject of trapping or better yet, some hands-on training. Perfect practice makes perfect.

Recommended reading on trapping: *Trappers Bible*

Rodents exist pretty much everywhere, so instead of using a commercial trap to satisfy your pest control needs, try crafting a deadfall.

Snares can be made with a piece of wire. However, professional snares with a locking mechanism are best. Some snare configurations hoist the animal into the air to prevent other critters from grabbing your groceries. Trapping isn't restricted to the land. We can also trap on and in the water.

Gill net

A gill net is a very productive means of sustenance acquisition. In a coastal area, a gill net would by my first course of action. You will be blessed with a variety of creatures when using this handy piece of kit…. birds, fish, turtles and many others.

Top: Construction of a gill net from Paracord. Bottom: The completed net is compact enough to fit in your hand.

Gill nets are commercially available, or you could make your own. Check your net at regular intervals and make repairs as needed. Save scraps and entrails from your catch for bait to use in your other traps or dump them next to your net to attract more aquatic life.

Note: Always check local regulations on the use of gillnets prior to setting one.

Bottle Trap

Sadly, plastic bottles are commonly found in many locations on earth. A savvy survivalist will capitalize on any of those available. By simply cutting off the upper portion, inverting it, and placing it into the main body of the bottle, you can easily catch bait and food. I have sustained myself by using six of these in tidal pools with no bait.

In freshwater streams, it is best to bait them. The small fish, crabs and crayfish caught in these can be made into a soup and eaten whole. Edible plant material can be added to such a soup to increase the nutritive value.

Bottle traps are easy to construct— simply cut the top of the bottle off just below the shoulder, invert it, and insert it into the bottle.

Foraging

For the purposes of this book, foraging will be defined as the gathering of plant matter and/or insects for sustenance.

Food is everywhere if only we slow down and look. A little knowledge helps as well. If a hunter spends three days in the field and returns empty handed, he has spent calories that he did not replace. If this pattern continues, death will be the final result. If it were possible to quantify the energy expended to produce and transport the food we currently consume, I believe we would find that the energy paid out would far surpass the energy imparted to the end user.

I had this epiphany over a bag of trail mix. As I read the list of ingredients, there were ten countries of origin represented. In my mind's eye, I envisioned the nuts and fruits being gathered and processed in ten separate locations from Chile to Africa. I then saw planes and ships moving the goods to a central location. Then, using plastics, electricity, machinery and human labor, a bag was produced.

The product was placed into bags, then into boxes. These boxes were transported yet again to a distribution center. Then the driver, using caloric energy and the most precious resource of all, time, drove the truck, using diesel fuel to pick up the product. After this, we see more time and energy spent to take the goods to the store at last.

But wait, there's more energy to pour out. Now we see the consumer, using caloric energy, time, money and fuel to retrieve what is ultimately, a snack! Look at all the energy that was spent to obtain a small bag of nuts and fruit. How many calories were in that bag? I'd say, not enough! If our ancestors lived as we do now, I fear we would have reached extinction long ago. Our current patterns of life will not last.

We call them *hunter-gatherers* for a reason, emphasis on *gatherer*.

Learn to forage. It is essential!

Bugs, slugs, worms, tree bark and plants can be eaten to keep your soul and body together. Such food sources often outperform "normal meats" on a nutritional level. Collectively, they can provide a healthful soup. All insects, worms and slugs should be cooked thoroughly before consumption as they often carry parasites that can be harmful to humans. So, it's always best to err on the side of caution.

Slugs

Slugs have been a steady part of my diet many times while living on the land. Wash your hands thoroughly after handling them as they can carry parasites. It is a good practice to put them in a vessel with some nontoxic vegetation and purge them for a few days. With that said, I have consumed slugs without purging them with no ill effects. You *must* cook them thoroughly. This last point is crucial. Slugs are known to carry meningitis and rat lungworm. Remember, purge them and boil or fry them thoroughly.

Don't be sluggish, give them a try.

Ants

Most species of ants are edible and delicious, some species even taste like lemons. According to Sara Ipatenco in an article updated on December 12, 2018, "A 3.5 ounce serving of red ants supplies about fourteen grams of protein," according to the National Geographic website. The same serving of red ants also supplies six milligrams of iron, which is seventy-one percent of the eight milligrams men need to consume daily and one-third of the eighteen milligrams women require on a daily basis. Ants are also a good source of calcium.

Take care when gathering ants though, some species have a fearsome bite.

Crickets

Crickets are enjoyed as a food source by many peoples the world over. I absolutely cook them as I regard them one of the more unclean creeping things. When cooked properly however, they are delicious with a mild nutty flavor and a pleasing aromatic bouquet. They pair well with a good cabernet sauvignon and pepper-jack cheese.

I have prepared these savory morsels on both a hot rock and in my trusty canteen cup. They must be moved about regularly to prevent them from sticking and burning. Once burned, the flavor changes into something most undesirable.

Earth Worms

In the study of nutrient content of earth worms consumed by the Ye'Kuana Amerindians of the Alto Orinoco of Venezuela, published January 10, 2003 in The Royal Society, the findings have value for the forager. Here are some highlights of the study.

"We analyzed eviscerated Kuru body proper, and whole and smoked preparations of "motto" for their content of protein and amino acids, fatty acids and twenty mineral and trace elements.

The samples contained large amounts of protein (64.5-72.9% of dry weight), essential amino acids, calcium and iron together with notable quantities of other important elements, indicating that these earth worms contain potentially useful quantities of many nutrients that are critical to the health of the humans who consume them."

Another section states: *"By comparing the essential amino acid content of a sample protein with that of the World Health Organization (WHO) standard protein, one can calculate the protein's chemical score and identify limiting amino acids in the nutritional source (table 2)* **In all cases, the earth worm proteins were of high quality, comparable with those of cow's milk and eggs** *(emphasis added by the authors)....*

"The content of arachidonic acids on a percentage basis in

these edible earthworms is very high when compared with that of some common foods, such as chicken, turkey, eggs and pork (figure 5)..."

In conclusion, the nutritional analyses reported here provide quantitative evidence to support the assertion that the earthworms consumed by the Ye'Kuana indigenous people of the Alto Orinoco are capable of satisfying a significant fraction of their daily requirements for essential amino acids and many of the trace metals, especially calcium and Iron."

Some folks advocate purging worms in a container. I don't really disagree but have never done so myself. Usually, if I'm eating worms, I'm really hungry, so I chop off the end and squeeze them out like toothpaste. I then roast them on a stone next to a fire or toss them into my ever-faithful canteen cup and make a soup. I have never noticed any ill effects consuming them.

Worms are prevalent in my area and they require little energy to gather. When fire is not an option, I have placed them on a rock and let the sun cook them, weather permitting. Worms are also a universally good bait for fishing and trapping. They can be dried and then ground into a flour and added to soups, stews or bread. In this way, they are unrecognizable as worms, thus the meal is more palatable to the more squeamish members of your party.

I have been unsuccessful in convincing my beautiful children that, "worms are good, you should try them; kids in other countries eat them all the time." However, they will try the soup though (Insert wicked laugh and sardonic grin here).

A worm farm could be added to the homestead to provide protein for the chickens and the people who inhabit it. I do recall reading some studies that indicate an earthworm's propensity to absorb heavy metals from the soil. As with all things, do your own research and take the most appropriate course of action.

In conclusion, whether it's a hillbilly such as myself eating worm soup in Appalachia or an African munching on a mopane worm, worms are good; they should be on your menu.

The Green Stuff

The use of plants for food and medicine is an integral part of the human story. The beauty of gathering plants for food lies in the fact that you need not club them in the head to secure sustenance and they don't run away.

It is not my intent to conduct an in-depth study of wild edibles. Such an undertaking would be beyond the scope of this book. Speaking of books, I generally do not learn well from them concerning plants. The bulk of my plant knowledge has been transmitted from the elders. That being said, one book I do enjoy, and we recommend, is Foragers Harvest by Samuel Thayer. There is no substitute for hands-on learning. Furthermore, plant life is most definitely a regionally specific study. Therefore, we strongly recommend that you seek out someone in your area that can guide you on your journey. Another option would be attending one of the reputable survival schools throughout the country, or attending a primitive skills gathering such as Rabbit Stick (https://www.rabbitstick.com/) or Earth Skills (http://www.earthskills.com/).

We offer these three plants to whet your appetite. The study of edible plants is definitely regionally specific. (See appendix for recommended reading).

Clover

Clover can be found in or near most all areas of human habitation or agriculture. Many children in rural communities have fed on it playfully to mimic the livestock, myself included. Clover can be eaten raw, but it is my belief that it should be boiled. I hold this belief based on the fact our digestive systems and enzymes differ from our animal brethren.

At times, the flower of the white clover is particularly sweet.

The flower of the red clover tastes similar to a raw green bean in my opinion and can be used as a medicine for blood purification, hormone stabilization and many other wonderful uses.

Clover.

Plantain.

Plantain

Plantain, most commonly found in both broad and narrow leaf varieties, is a plant well suited to thrive in disturbed soil areas. Plantain has a tightening, pulling, drawing, astringent effect. For this reason, is has been used for medicine by many peoples. When chewed and topically applied, plantain has historically been used for conditions ranging from stings to snakebite. The leaves can be eaten raw or cooked. I prefer cooked as they are less bitter after being prepared. Older plants can be stringy from the veins in the leaves. This can be off-putting but adds valuable fiber to the austere diet.

Pine Bark

From the Journal of Ethnobiology 29 (1): 94-112 spring/summer of 2009:
> *Bark Peeling, Food Stress and the Tree Spirits. The Use of Pine Inner Bark for Food in Scandinavia and North America.*

> *The old man (the Sun) showed them the roots and the berries and showed how to gather these; and certain times of the year, they should peel the bark of some trees and eat it... Black Feet creation (Grinell 1913).*

> *The Sami ate the inner bark of Scots pine fresh, roasted, or dried and ground into flour, which could be mixed with Reindeer milk, fat, blood or other food...*

> *Most studies of the Sami bark peeling have concluded that the Scots pine was not (emphasis added) an emergency food source, but rather a regularly collected and valued staple food (see Bergman et al, 2004; Nikalasson et al. 1994 Zackrisson et al 2004).*

> *Carbohydrates, vitamins, fiber and minerals are all important nutritional constituents in pine cambium. The carbohydrates helped balance the proteins and fat from meat, fish and Reindeer milk, the primary source of calories in the Sami diet, (Airaksinen et al, 1986, Hanson 1996). The relatively high vitamin C content of Scots pine inner bark probably prevented scurvy among the Sami; before the 19th century, scurvy was widespread among Swedish and Norwegian farm-*

ers living by the coast, but not among the Sami in the interior, (Fellman 1906; Urbye 1937).

Furthermore, inner bark contains beneficial food fiber, (Zackrisson et al, 2000) and high levels of iron and calcium, which was particularly important for healthy bone development and maintenance among children and pregnant women. Recent research shows that substances in Scots pine inner bark may reduce the risk of cardiovascular and cancer diseases, (Ostlund et al, 2004).

The nutritional qualities of inner bark make it particularly valuable in areas with significant seasonal variation in available plant foods. Inner bark contains a form of sugar in a fiber matrix, which reduces the rate of sugar absorption and keeps blood-sugar levels relatively steady for long periods. This makes it a good food for sustaining people during prolonged, high-energy activities, which may be why the Carrier ate pine bark during travels rather than carry stored food, (Lamb 1970). Energy is the most essential nutritional need. Therefore, sources of digestible carbohydrates that can be transformed into the glucose or other simple sugars have long been integral to the hunter-gatherer diets, and according to Flannery (1986), should be the highest priority foods in regions with sufficient protein resources. (emphasis added)

Speth and Spielman (1983) agree, suggesting that the hunter-gatherer in sharply seasonal environments generally needed to gather supplies of storable carbohydrates during fall stress in late winter and early spring. During these periods, protein was more available, and hence the primary sources of calories. But this diet was metabolically inefficient because proteins require more calories to metabolize than carbohydrates or fats and using proteins for energy could reduce skeletal muscle. Consequently, stored carbohydrates such as inner bark were important even when protein supplies were plentiful.

As you can see, considerable study has been done on the nutritive value of pine bark. If you harvest the bark correctly, the tree will remain unharmed. We must always strive to be good stewards of what we have been given.

Holding the blade with two hands like a draw knife ensures you will not harm the tree by cutting too deep. Only remove the bark from a narrow strip so the tree can recover.

Peeling the bark of white pine.

Use the blade of your knife to access the thin payer of cambium under the outer bark.

Properly done, peeling a section of bark from the tree will not harm it.

The nutritive content of the inner bark will vary depending upon when it is harvested. However, even in winter, it is worth the effort to obtain it. The needles can be steeped in hot water to create a healthful tea. This tea is rich in vitamin C, an essential nutrient.

Why is vitamin C important? First, we must understand that vitamin C is a water-soluble vitamin. As such, your body does not produce or store it. *You must have a daily source* to maintain optimal health. Additionally, Vitamin C, or the lack thereof, can impact everything from your skin to your teeth, even your immune system!

One of our favorite methods to prepare pine bark is to peel it into strips and roast it by a fire, bush potato chips! It imparts a pleasant nutty flavor with a satisfying crispiness. Do not underestimate the value of food texture to the survivor! To stay properly fed, you will most likely need to hunt, fish, trap, forage and grow your own food. Not to mention utilizing your food stores. Just like a solid financial portfolio, you must diversify your grocery grabbin' capabilities.

9 - The Homestead

The greatest fine art of the future will be the making of
a comfortable living from a small piece of land.
—Abraham Lincoln

T HERE HAS BEEN MUCH DISCUSSION in the preparedness/ survival community concerning "bugging out". This is only a temporary solution, the idea being to transport oneself and family from a dangerous situation to a more stable one. Much has been said of making the trek to a "bug-out location" or "retreat".

I fear many would perish in such an attempt if the distance were far or, the time afoot more than a few days. The most desirable situation is to already be living in your retreat and making progress towards a more self-sufficient lifestyle. Food infrastructure takes time to build. I favor low maintenance options. For example, blueberries thrive in my area. They require very little energy expenditure on my part, yet they provide a powerhouse of nutrients.

Constructing raised beds is a good step toward agricultural bliss. Raised beds have the additional benefit of being easier to perform work in than rows on the ground. This is especially true for those of us with back troubles and the elderly. Raised beds also afford the ability to focus our fertilization in a more concentrated way.

Additionally, raised beds, when properly constructed and strategi-cally placed, can produce a defensive position to fend off the unsavory bi-peds. The initial outlay of labor and material cost may be a limiting factor for some.

Obviously, water and food production are linked, therefore it is essential to secure your water supply. If a well is to be used, it is imperative that an alternate system be installed to ensure the ability to pump water, independent of the power grid. Solar power and hand pumps are good options. Rain catchment options should also be considered.

Raised beds.

Security and food are intimately connected. If you and your tribe are not getting enough to eat, you won't be very effective in performing security-related tasks. Also, the very possession of food stores and a homestead will guarantee your status as a potential target. Living in your retreat before festivities commence is your best hope for survival.

Most modern homes built in the United States are completely impractical, especially from a security standpoint. I have seen many doors made of glass in this country. This is total stupidity! Many walls today consist only of thin vinyl siding, Styrofoam, plywood and sheetrock. These walls will not stop bullets or even an angry dude with a tomahawk, plan accordingly! The quest to feed yourself and those who depend on you is a never-ending challenge. Foresight is essential in this undertaking; prepare now!

Chickens are a great livestock option. They require less care than large animals and produce food without having to slaughter them. Once they've aged out of laying, they can then be slaughtered for the pot.

Protecting your livestock is crucial. A good dog, like Aslan, a Great Pyrenees will not only protect the animals but can be good intruder detection.

You must lay in a *deep* supply of food for your family. You must begin now to produce, preserve and store your own food to the greatest extent possible, given your circumstances. You must be able to defend it all, so that you and yours maintain control of what you have worked so hard to amass. Remember, you must be able to hunt, trap and forage to supplement what the homestead provides. These skills will also serve you well if your home is destroyed or overrun. Each skill set discussed herein has many nuances. No one is coming to save you. There is much to do, and there is no substitute for hands-on experience. Go get some. Now.

If you're not already living this lifestyle, there will be a steep learning curve. Game day is not the time to learn to garden! Buying a seed vault or two from Amazon and tossing it into the back of the closet and considering it your plan to feed your family will probably result in you watching them slowly starve to death.

A milking stand makes the job of milking the goats much easier. They become accustomed to the process and immediately walk up onto the stand for their turn.

10 - Bug Out Bag

By failing to prepare, you are preparing to fail.
—Benjamin Franklin

T HERE HAS BEEN SO MUCH discussion on this topic, I hesitate to even utter the phrase anymore. Bug out this, bug out that, blah, blah, blah. However, no book on survival or prepared-ness would be considered complete without at least mentioning it, so here we go.

For the purpose of this book, we shall define a "bug-out" as the act of transporting oneself and/or one's companions from an unsafe location to a safer location. I will not provide you with a list of items to place in said bag. I don't presume to know you, your situation, where you live or what season we're talking about. I will, however, give you my thoughts on the matter.

Generally speaking, I think entirely too much energy goes into this topic. If I am within a day's walk of my home or any other location that makes me feel warm and fuzzy, I don't need no stinking bag.

Remember all that stuff we discussed in the EDC section? I have everything I need in my pockets and on my person. My area is so well blessed with water that I can't walk a straight line without tripping over a creek.

However, if I'm on a long road trip, I do pack what may be referred to as an INCH bag (I'm Never Coming Home). If an EMP strikes and

I'm a few hundred miles from home, I'm probably going to remain there with my friends and try to be useful to that community. On the other hand, if I'm halfway home and things go kinetic, I'm in quite a pickle. I don't know anyone for hundreds of miles. If I'm traveling alone, I won't have anyone to keep watch as I sleep. If I'm traveling with my kids, I would probably use the rope in the back of my vehicle to hang myself from the nearest tree because even Job himself ain't got that kind of patience (just kidding), but it would complicate things.

Let's assume I'm alone. My first course of action would be to quickly gather the useful and practical items from my vehicle, so long as they won't slow me down. Remember, I have to carry all this crap. I sling my INCH bag over my shoulder and start walking. People are in shock. I'm on the interstate, there are plenty of folks standing around looking at their phones wondering what's happening. My phone doesn't work anymore. I heard a man near me say the same. My radar is starting to go off, things aren't ok, and everyone knows it. My instincts tell me to get away from people. People are dangerous, the woods are relatively safe. Off I go.

As I look around, it seems no one notices me, so I slink off into the tree line. It will be dark soon. As I was driving, I just kinda checked out, jamming to some tunes on the radio. I'm not sure of my exact location. Two hundred yards in, I notice a thicket of briar and bramble. No normal person will pass through here, I think. That's exactly where I need to be. I turn around to see if I have left any signs of my passing. The soil is dry, I see no visible tracks, so I drop down to my hands and knees and carefully crawl into this hell of lacerating vegetation.

After crawling a considerable distance, I feel confident that no human will stumble upon my position. It's getting pretty dark now, so I decide to hunker down.

I roll the pack off of my shoulders quietly, slowly, and place it carefully on the ground. I withdraw my Ruger 10-22 Takedown rifle and smoothly assemble it, insert the magazine and chamber a fresh round of ammunition and put the weapon on safe. Some folks may say that a .22 caliber is underpowered, but I don't want to be shot with one, especially in the face. Twenty-two ammo is light, so I can carry plenty of it without carrying too much weight. I recently checked the zero on both my iron sight and my Leupold scope, then I cleaned and lubricated my rifle. It's ready. I also have my Glock, chambered in 9 mm with three extra magazines, as the Lord hath commanded. I have my knife. If trouble comes, I'll be ready. I'm not looking for a fight. I just want to sleep and figure out what's next.

Fortunately, I had the foresight to pack six perimeter alarms. They fire a 209 shotgun primer when the trip wire is breached, so I string them around the area where I intend to sleep. This should wake me up in time to respond to an approaching threat. I take my PVS 14 out and place it into the "skull crusher" mount. I pop in a fresh battery and turn it on to be sure it's working. It's ready if something goes bump in the night.

The weather is tolerable, so I just spread my poncho on the ground. I place my Gore-Tex bivy sack, along with a poncho liner on half, crawl inside and pull the other half over me like a taco. If something happens and I need to move, I can cram all this in my pack quickly and run like hell. I don't use the zipper on the bivy sack; I don't want to be trapped inside. I sleep with my boots and clothing on so I can jump to my feet if the need arises.

I notice a partial moon, so I remove anything that may reflect light and give away my position. My eyes are heavy, I drift off to sleep.

Morning comes, I awaken and just lie quiet and still. I use all my senses to dial in. I look, listen, smell and feel the world around me. It seems safe to emerge from my chrysalis, so I do so slowly and quietly, placing my bedding in my pack while still giving heed to all my senses.

Before moving from this spot, I scan the area to be sure that I have left no spoor. I cautiously move to a small hill with a view of the interstate. I avoid the top of the hill; this prevents my silhouette from being visible to the folks below. I take a knee and withdraw a map.

I pull out my trusty Steiner binoculars and have a look towards the interstate. I can see mile marker 316. After looking at the map, I can see that the halfway point between my current location and my home is roughly the area of Memphis, Tennessee. Memphis is the home of Elvis Presley. A city of that size is potentially dangerous at night, which is when I'll be doing most of my walking. I'll have to be careful. Now that the grid is down, I can only imagine the chaos. Memphis is located next to the Mississippi River. That means I'll probably need to utilize a bridge to cross it or go for a swim.

I hate my life. I'm pretty far from home but I've got some skills. I have seen and done some things, but I'm far, far away from home. I'm honestly a little scared. I'm a solid dude, but I'm also a realist. My current situation sucks woefully.

I know that the interstate will take me home, but I can't walk along the roadside. People are there, some walking, some lost in despair. People equal problems, so I need to be a ghost. Humans are creatures of habit. They tend to cling to a known location during hours of darkness. People always establish patterns of life. I must do the opposite of what they do. Based on my observations in this location, the majority of people tend to chill out about 1 am. They begin to stir around 6 am. That's a five-hour window. People are visibly shaken and sleeping eight hours is about to become a thing of the past for most. So, between the hours of 1-6 am, I will proceed along my route. I will use the interstate as a handrail, I will maintain loose visual contact with it, while remaining in the trees.

I think I'll just sit right here and wait for night to fall. This will give me a chance to observe the road and get a feel for what's going on. Hours pass. I'm a little hungry but I don't eat. I need to lose a couple of pounds anyway. My more pressing need is water. I have two quarts with me, but it won't last long. I take a drink and keep watching. I've heard a few gunshots, sounded like sidearms. People are becoming increasingly fearful; it's palpable.

Darkness comes. I stand up and begin moving slowly. I've been walking for about three hours now. Moving quietly is very difficult; dry leaves cover the ground; tree limbs and briars are everywhere tearing at me. It's going to take a long, long time to get home moving like this. After walking another hour or so, I see a couple of fires burning.

They look like campfires. It's an exit ramp and an overpass. People are packed under the overpass, using it for shelter. They got tired of walking, I guess.

The wind shifts towards me. I can smell the wood smoke mixed with the scent of tobacco and human waste. A few guys are talking, passing around a large bottle.

A child is crying at the top of their lungs, not close to me but off in the distance. It sounds like an infant. I've got four kids; I know that sound. My thoughts drift to my children. I can see their faces; I can smell them. Are they okay? Will I ever see them again? Tears begin to form. I choke them back. *Get your mind straight*, I tell myself. "You gotta stay focused", I whisper aloud. I keep stepping.

"You better swing wide around this," I tell myself. I begin drifting to my left. A road comes into view; to the right, it leads back to the overpass.

I don't know what's to the left. It doesn't matter, it's the wrong direction anyway. I need to cross this road. As I come near it, I take a knee and carefully look in both directions. I'm listening intently. I have chosen a bend in the road with a slight depression as the best place to cross. I am concealed by vegetation as I look things over. It feels safe to cross so I do it quickly. I dash into the woods on the other side about fifty yards deep and again take a knee to look, listen and feel. After about 10 minutes, I'm not seeing or hearing anything, so I keep walking.

The world is starting to come alive slowly, by degrees. The light is changing. I need to find a place to bed down.

Off in the distance I see a huge, very rickety old barn with junk lying around. Obviously, this place isn't being used and hasn't been for a long time. I'm not going to use it for a shelter though. It looks like the barn is sitting right up against the property line represented by the barbed wire. The barn was once surrounded by pasture. Now, weeds and saplings emerge from where the cows once grazed.

On the other side of the fence is the nastiest, most God forsaken hell of briars and tangled vegetation I have ever seen. It's perfect! Ahh, yes ma'am, I'll be checking into the Thorny Inn. I have reservations, the name is Sasquatch, party of one.

I burrow into this prickly den and tune into my surroundings before setting up shop. It's much brighter now. My hands, arms and face are scratched and bloody from all my walking. I'm tired, thirsty, hungry and sore. Sleep comes quickly.

I awaken in the late afternoon; my mouth is so dry I think I could strike matches on my tongue. My back hurts. My feet hurt. I smell like a load of wet towels left in the washing machine to sour.

Unscrewing the lid on my canteen, I savor the last of my water. I crawl out of the thicket. It's not dark yet, but I really need to find some water. I will be hypervigilant not to be seen. Farms, especially old ones, are usually located near water. Cows gotta drink too.

Ahh yes, there's the pond! This one has a small spring feeding into it. I'll get my water there. Running the water through my filter, I top off both one-quart canteens and my water bladder. As soon as I'm finished, I move back into the trees. A pine thicket comes into view, so I go there. It isn't dark enough yet to start walking and I think I'll have a bite to eat. I select a small envelope of tuna. Hmm, says here it's "dolphin safe." Well that sucks, I rather fancy a chunk of dolphin now and then. I pour some cold water into a pouch of instant potatoes and stir it up. Something starchy would be good right about now. I don't bother trying to cook it. I scarf it all down.

My food won't last long enough for me to make it home. I've seen a few squirrels and a rabbit. I could set some traps, but that takes time and I want to move as quickly as possible. I have my .22 caliber rifle and I'll probably stumble across something to put in the pot. The problem is if I shoot, everyone within earshot will know I'm around. I'm not to the point where I need to shoot anything yet, but I want to be ready. Daylight surrenders to darkness; once again I'm on the move…

Day 7—My food is all gone. Luckily, I know lots of edible plants, so I have been snacking on the go to keep my strength up. Thankfully, water resupply hasn't been an issue. One day, I used my Silcox key to get some water from a building. I'm glad I packed it. Surprisingly, enough water came out to fill both canteens, barely. The flow was just a trickle, so it took a bit of time. I knew approaching a structure was risky, but I was really thirsty. I'm not feeling well today. I had some pretty severe diarrhea just after sunup. I took an Imodium tablet out of my med kit and sipped a little water. I'll see what happens...

Day 11—A few days back I got pretty sick, too sick to keep walking. I found a good layup position and alternated between bouts of vomiting and rapid spontaneous bowel evacuations for the better part of two days. Then a thunderstorm rolled in on top of me. The rain pelted me like it was personal. The winds were intense! A couple trees came down one night so close that I felt the ground shake. The temperature cooled a bit after that. I was saturated in a mix of rainwater and bodily fluids. I wasn't dead, but I sure smelled that way. I managed to get to some fresh water and clean myself up as best I could.

While I was cleaning up, I noticed a tick on me bollocks. Over three-quarters of the tick's body was embedded inside me. I tugged on it some. I felt cutting it out was the only way to remove all of it. I haven't worked up the nerve yet. *(This actually happened to me once. Luckily, I had a doctor in the field with me. He cut out the tick without the benefit of using anything to numb the pain. Four days after returning home, I developed a fever and was prescribed doxycycline. I still cannot look Doc squarely in the eye when I see him. Yeah, living in the woods is great fun!)* I've been back on the move for about a day now.

Day 12—Last night while I was walking, I caught the sharp end of a dead, dry tree limb in my right eye. It hurt like hell. When I pulled my hand away it was wet with blood and tears. I folded up a gauze pad and made an eye patch for myself; first I irrigated the wound then I secured the gauze with a bandanna. After sunrise, I removed the eyepatch and had a look with my signal mirror. I'm no doctor, but it looks bad. There was enough moonlight to walk by, but not enough to see that branch. What's more, I can't see anything clearly out of that eye now!

I'm tripping over things and making more noise as a result. My depth perception must be off. I checked my map yesterday and I haven't traveled as far as I had hoped. Moving stealthily is a marathon, not a sprint. Somedays, I have to go well out of my way to avoid danger. At this rate, it will take an eternity to make it home. Everything has been much harder than I *ever* thought it would be.

Day 14—I'm moving through a wooded area between a subdivision and a tract of land that seems to be a mom and pop type farm. I have no energy. Being on the move, carrying this pack, is taking its toll. The fact that I'm eating very little isn't helping matters at all. The sun is on the horizon. I need a place to lay up.

Suddenly, a dog appears out of nowhere and begins barking incessantly. I try to move away but he follows, barking louder and more intensely. Four men wearing farmer type clothing appear out of nowhere. They are all armed with a mixture of shotguns and deer rifles. One of the men is older than the rest. The other three are his sons or sons-in-law I figure. The dog is still barking intensely.

"There!" The eldest man shouts as he indicates my location by pointing his Winchester 30-30 at me. "He's got a gun!" yells the muscular one with the red beard.

"I'm not looking for any trouble, I'm just..." Boom! Fire spews from the patriarch's rifle. All the men start moving. I drop my pack and run for all I'm worth. He missed me; I think. The dog and the men are running close behind me now. I think of turning and firing but they are too close, I might get one, but the others would get me for sure.

As I top the small hill before me, my right leg buckles underneath my body and I tumble. My upper thigh is bloody. I guess he didn't miss after all. As soon as I saw the wound, searing pain enveloped my body. How could I have been shot and not know it? Somehow, I'm on my feet again trying to run. Looking back, I can't see the men now. They must be using the large tree trunks for cover. Boom! Boom! My left shoulder blade feels like it's on fire. I stumble over the hilltop only to find a drop-off on the other side. I realized it too late as my body tumbles and bounces, tumbles and bounces. Gravity always wins. I came to rest on a sharp rock. The area just below the base of my skull took most of the impact. I'm not hurting anymore. In fact, I can't move anything with the exception of my good eye.

I shift my eye up and to the left. The men are standing on the crest of the hill, looking down at me. "I'm tired of these sum bitches comin' on our land," says red beard. "Yep," the elder replies.

Those are the last words I will ever hear. A peaceful feeling of warmth washes over me, then darkness.

This was, of course, a short work of fiction. I've lived long enough to know that most people's fantasy of a long-range bug-out is self-delusion. Thank you for indulging me in that brief digression. It began as a mental exercise and I just started writing it down, and before I knew what happened. Voila! So, here's my theory on what a bag should do. It should contain the items essential to transport you and/or your companions from an unsafe location to a more secure location. This theory is, of course, predicated upon the belief that a journey of hundreds of miles is an unrealistic goal.

In planning your bug-out, you must ask yourself the following questions:

- How long will my journey last?
- What is the terrain/climate/season?
- Can I resupply water en route?
- What actions must I perform en route?
- Is the weight of my pack realistic for me?
- Do I possess the skills to improvise in the absence of equipment?
- Are there any special considerations? (infants, essential medications such as insulin, etc.)

Let's assume the location of your employment is 50 miles from where you live. (According to ABC news, the average American drives 16 miles to work each day).

You're at work when the bad thing happens. Driving home isn't an option. You have prepared a bug-out bag that you keep in your car. It's summertime. Given your current state of fitness and considering the terrain, along with the safest route home, you conclude that you will be able to travel 10 miles per day. That's an expected travel time of five days afoot. What items will you require for a five-day hike? You will obviously need to hydrate. Water is heavy. If water resupply points are available along your route, you are truly blessed; that's less you'll have to carry. You will want to sleep, ideally in a dry condition, in optimal temperature, free from insects. Some food would be nice, let's plan on one meal per day. You might run into trouble, a pistol along with a knife would be the bare minimum. A solid pair of comfortable shoes or hiking boots that have *already been broken in*, should accompany your pack. Those dress shoes you wear in the cubicle simply won't do. You will probably have a bowel movement within the space of 5 days so a handful of baby wipes would be a welcome addition. You will want to keep a low profile, so making a fire would only be done as necessity dictates.

No kit would be complete without the ability to make fire, so let's add some cotton balls mixed with Vaseline, a butane lighter and a ferrocerium rod as a backup. It might rain. Instead of packing a rain suit, let's use the time tested and proven military style poncho; they can be found in various colors and patterns to fit your specific needs while maintaining a discreet appearance. In addition to keeping you and your pack from getting soaked, a poncho can turn your pack in to a flotation device. It can also be fashioned into a shelter, rainwater catch or a litter to carry an injured person. Ponchos are light weight and highly versatile. I always carry one in any kit I build. A metal container is an essential piece of kit. No pack would be complete without one and they are very hard to improvise. While a pot may not be essential within the span of a five-day hike, I would pack one anyway, just in case the ordeal goes longer than expected. At a bare minimum, I would carry a stainless-steel water bottle and/or metal cup.

A quality compass along with maps of the area would be a wise choice. Hopefully, you have done your homework and have chosen more than one route to use on your journey home, while factoring in your personal security and water resupply.

Cordage would be a good idea to have in your bag. I carry many small sections of 550, AKA parachute cord.

The pack itself should be comfortable and adjusted to fit you. I prefer earth-tone colors, while avoiding an overly "militaristic" appearance.

Bug Out Bag

In the survival community, it has often been said, "The more you know, the less you have to carry." I suppose that's essentially true, but only to a point. I have done the primitive stone age thing. It's a good idea to possess those skills to fall back on in the absence of all else. There's a reason we no longer use stone tools, they are woefully inadequate when compared to metal ones. I would much rather take my chances on a hunt with a .22 caliber rifle and scope instead of a throwing stick. An effective primitive shelter can take hours to build, so why would I not just carry some shelter with me? Less expenditure of time and calories means success in my view. I'm not advocating forsaking primitive earth skills, quite the opposite,

I think everyone should know them. I also think if you find yourself HAVING to rub sticks together to make a fire, you have failed in the area of planning and preparedness.

Every situation will differ, the preceding was intended as fuel for thought and a template of how you can approach the issue of building a pack that's right for you. At the end of the day, you will live or die by the choices you make, so CHOOSE WISELY!

11 - The Chariot

The car has become the carapace, the protective and aggressive shell, of urban and suburban man.
—Marshal McLuhan

T HE PERSONAL VEHICLE HAS BECOME an integral part of daily life. These machines have replaced the trusty steeds, chariots and wagons of the past. Generally speaking, we interact with, and are transported by them on a daily basis. They are our modern beasts of burden, enabling us to travel and carry things more efficiently than we could with our own physical power. When the majority of people start up the engine and begin their daily travels, they give little thought to what may happen. Our previous daily patterns have established an expectation that this will be just another day. Everything will be normal. At some point later that same day, we assume we will return to our homes and sleep in a comfortable bed.

In January 2014, an incident dubbed Snowpocalypse occurred which led to thousands of motorists being stranded in bumper-to-bumper traffic. Hundreds of traffic accidents were reported. Thousands of flights were canceled with hundreds of others delayed. School children were stranded overnight and forced to sleep in classrooms. Many people slept in their cars. Many others abandoned their cars and took shelter in stores and restaurants. Roads quickly became clogged and impassable. Abandoned cars littered roads and the interstates.

I recall watching the news on television in my native Georgia. The city of Atlanta was among the greatly affected areas. One reporter highlighted the story of a young lady who was pregnant and stranded in her vehicle. She also had a young child in the back seat. What provisions did she have available? Breath mints. Yes, breath mints, that was it. Thank goodness she was ultimately given a ride by a good Samaritan. We're talking less than three inches of snow and ice! The city was essentially crippled.

I think this young lady's level of preparedness is indicative of the average American's lack of readiness. Instances such as this are why this book was written. I'm glad it ended well for the young lady and her children!

Generally speaking, our vehicle is our nearest resupply point. Think about it. As I write this, I can look through the window and see my vehicle parked outside my home. Earlier today, I drove into town using that vehicle. As I entered different buildings conducting my business and errands, my vehicle was the closest thing that I could control. What's inside?

- Water (five gallon can)
- Three-day food supply
- Flashlight/headlamp w/spare batteries
- Sleeping bag/wool blankets
- Axe
- Shovel
- 100 feet of rope
- Medical kit (along with knowledge)
- Jumper cables
- Basic tool kit
- A GOOD jack (not the one that came with the vehicle)
- Four-way lug wrench
- An extra spare tire (total of two)
- Snow chains
- A couple of books
- A current road atlas
- A backpack (BOB, INCH bag, call it what you want)
- Essential medications if needed

Sounds like a lot? It is. Too much? Overkill? I don't think so. Experience hath shown otherwise...

I can carry all of this without detracting from the passenger capacity of five people. That number works for me. Additionally, I still have enough room for groceries, etc. On occasion, I do have to shuffle things around, but that's ok. You will not find me ill equipped in a snowstorm or any other occurrence which might compel me to slumber in my vehicle for a few days.

Water

For my situation/location, one Jerry can of water is sufficient. If you live in a desert, obviously carry as much water as possible. In urban areas, it may also be wise to lay in additional water since safe sources of water may not be available.

Food

A three-day supply of food is an absolute minimum. Vehicles can become really hot in the summer; this can accelerate the degradation of food and other supplies, so be sure to cycle them out at regular intervals. I prefer foods that do not require cooking. If you plan to cook, simply include the means to do so (outside of the vehicle). Consider who you may be feeding. If you carpool with coworkers, you must factor in food allergies and religious limitations. Preference matters as well. One of my beloved children is quite finicky; she may well choose to perish rather than consume things that "her majesty" deems beneath her palate. Speaking of kids, consider including *fun* foods to boost morale.

Everyone in my bloodline falls into the category of hopeless chocoholics. Chocolate doesn't fare well in the heat though, so I use dehydrated cocoa mix for the kids. For myself, a mixture consisting of equal parts vodka and chocolate syrup will surely see me though any calamity.

Flashlight/Headlamp

A source of light is a handy item. Flashlights are good, I carry a few. However, their operation demands the use of one hand. This is not optimal when changing a tire or performing first-aid tasks. A headlamp will provide hands-free illumination where you need it. I highly recommend this addition to your vehicle kit.

Sleeping Bags

Sadly, people can easily die from exposure even when using a vehicle as shelter. If the fuel runs out (a good reason to never let your fuel drop below half a tank, which is my personal practice), the heater is no longer an option. A sleeping bag or woolen blanket, along with the proper clothing for each member of you family is absolutely essential.

Axe

With the exception of water, I have used the axe more than any other piece of equipment I carry. Many times, I have rounded a curve or topped a hill only to be confronted by a line of cars. What's the holdup? A tree or large branch has fallen across the road. I get out, axe in hand and fix the problem. On one such occasion, a deputy was there, and he told me that the highway department was on the way, but they wouldn't be coming any time soon as other trees were down across the county. I told him to call them off, I would handle this one.

At the time, I was driving a Dodge truck and it just so happened that I had a chainsaw with me. I took out the saw and went to work. Very quickly, the saw ceased to function. It was beyond the scope of available tools and parts to bring it back to life. Without hesitation, I returned to my truck and pulled out my axe. Low technology rarely fails. I set to chopping the tree into manageable sections. Large chunks of wood flew as I worked. I keep my axe razor sharp and I have used one since my youth.

Two older gentlemen clad in overalls and work boots stood along the roadside and watched as I worked. I heard one say, "That's a sharp axe!" To which the other replied, "Look what's swinging it!" (I stand six feet six inches tall and weighed 250 pounds then) I chuckled hearing this. Shortly, the branches had been removed and the trunk reduced to manageable sections. The two older gents along with the deputy and a few other bystanders pulled the branches out of the road as I removed the more cumbersome sections. With the work done, I returned my axe to its Kydex sheath with a melodious click. I shook hands with the men and drove away. The line of motorists had grown since my arrival, none of them had an axe though. The deputy was now free to handle other business and traffic resumed in a normal fashion.

More recently, oddly enough, as I was driving down to Chris Weatherman's house to begin our collaboration on this very book, I encountered another tree. Many cars were lined up this time in both directions. There had been no storm or high winds, maybe the tree just got tired and decided to call it quits. A few people had gotten out of their vehicles to assess the situation, yet no one was taking any action.

Once again, I pulled Excalibur from the stone and began chopping the tree in half, the double yellow line between my feet. With that cut made, I returned to my chariot, returned the axe to its sheath and drove around the other vehicles, coming to a stop close to the tree. I took out my rope, tied one end to the tree and other to my vehicle. I pulled the first half until it was clear of the roadway. After having a few people relocate their vehicles, I repeated the process on the other half as before. As I was coiling up my rope, I heard a woman in the crowd say, "At least somebody was prepared!" Once again, I was the only one with an axe. There have been several other occasions in which my axe was put to use clearing the path while others stood by waiting for someone, (someone else) to do something.

I'm not quite finished telling you about my axe experiences. I recall two other times when my axe was put to, uhhh, more unconventional use. I was driving through a parking lot between a grocery store and a pharmacy when I noticed a young lady I'd once worked with. I hadn't seen her in years but could tell something was wrong, her face told the tale.

"Hey, long time no see, how are you?" I asked.

"Well, I've locked my keys in the car and I have a baby in the backseat," she replied.

I walked up to the car and had a look. Luckily, the baby was sleeping peacefully in her car seat. My eyes shifted to the car's locks. "I can get you in," I replied confidently.

I walked over to a bush at the parking lot's edge, withdrew my knife and removed a branch that was reasonably straight. I chose a section of the branch about four feet long and roughly the size of a pencil. Using my knife, I removed all the secondary branches and made the whole stick smooth. She looked on quizzically as I trimmed the stick.

"Is she still sleeping?" I asked concerning the baby. "Yes," she replied.

"Good."

I returned to my vehicle and fetched my axe. Her eyes were wide in a mixture of shock and disbelief as I drew near with an axe in one hand and a stick in another. "Oh wait," she said. I began laughing and through my laughter I said, "No, it's okay, I'm not going to smash anything."

I placed the cutting edge of the axe into the crack between the top of the door and the roof of the car, axe handle parallel to the ground. Grasping the axe with one hand, I began to pry gently and the space between the top edge of the door and the roof of the car widened. With my other hand, I inserted the stick through the gap until the tip hovered just above the button of the lock control. Then with a carefully aimed gentle push, "click". The doors were unlocked. I carefully withdrew the stick and the axe. "Voila," I said as I opened the door. The baby was still sleeping.

So, here we have bushcraft, preparedness and creativity combined and applied to solve a problem. No damage was done to the car. No infants were harmed during the incident. Everybody wins.

I hesitate to the tell the next one, as it may be unpleasant to some, but here goes. One evening, I was driving home. The sun was settling on the horizon as a car came into view. This car wasn't totally off the road, but it wasn't exactly on it either. As I drew nearer, I could see two teenage girls standing at the front bumper looking down. I stopped and got out to see what was happening and offer assistance.

As I walked around the front of the car, I saw a deer badly damaged from the collision. Its feeble attempts to move made it obvious that the rear half of its body was paralyzed. The blood that bubbled from the nose and mouth told me that the internal damage was extensive. I intuitively knew this creature was dying. Anyone who knows me can attest to the fact that I despise suffering. Sometimes in life you have to kill; that's part of it, just do it quickly.

After a moment of watching, I knew what had to be done. I walked back to my car (a Honda Accord at that time) and took out the axe and approached the deer from behind where it wouldn't have to see it coming. I muttered the words I'm sorry under my breath. There is a communication that transcends language and species. He became still and a feeling washed over me that he not only understood but welcomed the relief he knew I would give. The axe struck as intended, just below the skull, severing all communication of pain. The girls shrieked at this. I had forgotten that they were there, being lost in other worldly communication with a brother creature. I placed him in the trunk and carried him to a man I knew, who lived about ten miles down the road. He had five children at home then and a wife that was about half Cherokee. I laid the deer at his feet, telling him the story. Before our conversation had ended, the deer was being skinned by his wife and one of the children. His wife commented on what she would do with the hide and hooves, nothing would go to waste. It was a good death.

Shovel

A small shovel can be a real asset in some tire-changing situations. Such a tool can also be pressed into service as a formidable weapon for self-preservation. Some may choose a folding model; they work just fine. The one

I currently carry is a model patterned after the Russian Spetznaz shovel, AKA Russian death spoon.

Once while in the Pacific Northwest, I was talking with members of the homeless community. These people can teach us a lot. While talking to a man named Clarence, I asked him, "If you could have one item to help you in your daily life, what would that be?" His answer was immediate and surprising. "A folding shovel, so I could be clean."

Clarence went on to list the things he could accomplish with this simple tool, from burying his waste to keeping his camp clean. Don't underestimate the humble shovel. Or socks for that matter. Clarence was very passionate about those as well.

Rope

I generally carry about a hundred feet of rope. I live in the mountains; one never knows what life will throw at a person up here. You may not need or want that much. It's your call. But please carry something that enables you to pull a vehicle out of a ditch or off of the road. A chain or tow strap may also suffice.

One day, my eldest son came to visit. The visit concluded, we hugged and said goodbye. Approximately five minutes after his departure, my phone rang.

"Hey Dad, I'm stuck."

"Where are you, son?"

"Just down the hill, first road on the left."

"I'm on my way."

I arrived at the scene chuckling as one does when their teenage boy does things that remind them of mishaps that they themselves had around that same age. A miscalculation on his part had placed one of his tires into the drainage ditch with no hope of traction or extraction. I pulled out my rope, tethered one vehicle to the other and gave instructions to the fruit of my loins as to his part of the procedure. Voila! Liberation and humiliation simultaneously.

"I've told you to always be ready, you might want to get a rope, son."

"Yeah, I know, love you, Dad."

"Love you too, son."

Medical Kit

It has been my misfortune to find myself in need of medical equipment on more than one occasion, usually on the behalf of others. Like my friend Skinny Medic says, "You never know when you will be the first responder." On a sunny day as I was traveling down a mountain road, I rounded one of the many curves and saw a motorcycle up against a tree. The unfortunate rider was sitting on the roadside where his body came to a stop, after sliding quite some distance. Noticeably absent was the skin and muscle tissue that once covered the palms of his hands and inner forearms.

I quickly dressed his injuries and wrapped him in a mylar blanket. A man stopped at the scene and offered to drive him to the hospital. There was no cellular service on the mountain and even if there were, driving him from the scene was the fastest way to get him the care he needed.

On another occasion, I was going down a slide in a park with my youngest son. As we made the final turn at the end of the slide, his left foot caught the edge, twisting his foot sharply in a counterclockwise fashion. When he attempted to stand, it was obvious he wasn't comfortable putting his weight on his left foot. I checked him out, looking first for any signs of an obvious break. I found none but knew that a hairline or stress fracture was a possibility. As previously stated, the vehicle is always the closest resupply point. I took the medical kit from the car and fashioned my SAM splint into an improvised cast to immobilize both the ankle and knee. After that, I applied a cold compress.

After a visit to the ER, an x-ray confirmed a minor spiral tib/fib fracture. I'm proud to say the tough lad has made a full recovery.

On several other occasions, the medical kit kept in my vehicle has been used as I encountered everything from automobile accidents to minor cuts. On more than one occasion, I noticed a pattern. People freeze up. One morning while eating breakfast with my children at a local restaurant, a man collapsed from his bar stool, bouncing as he struck the floor. The restaurant was packed. Everyone fell silent and just looked at the man. No one was making any effort to do anything.

"Watch my kids please," I said to the waitress as I stood up. "Man, fall down, chair!" my talkative youngest son kept parroting, "man, fall down, chair!" That was the only sound in the place. Everyone was in shock. I turned to the owner, "Call 911," I said. I then turned to a lady seated near me and repeated this request separately to her to be sure the call would be made.

My initial impression was that the man was dead. Shortly after checking his airway for obstructions, securing it and giving him the unpleasant sternal rub, he slowly came around. I saw no medical alert jewelry. I kept him in a stable position and continued to access his level of consciousness while checking him for secondary injuries from his fall. Paramedics were on the scene quickly, I bowed out and returned to my pancakes. No one did anything! They all froze! I have seen this very thing happen numerous times! From my perspective, it shatters the myth that most people believe and tell themselves, "I will rise to the occasion when something bad happens." I don't think so. My observations of people in abnormal, scary situations has convinced me that the opposite is true. Most will freeze.

Why does it seem that I am always the first to act? I'm really not sure but I think a couple of things may be a factor. I have some training under my belt. I may not be the best man for the job, but many times I have been the only one available and willing at the time. Secondly, my mindset is different than the average guy, not better, just different. I don't suffer from normalcy bias. I go through life everyday with the awareness of, *yes, it can happen to you. And it may happen today.*

In another time, in another country, I worked really hard to save a man's life. Ultimately, he didn't make it. There were in excess of thirty people standing around, in shock, doing nothing. I'm not sure how long he had been without an airway before I arrived. I learned a few lessons that day. Chief among them, people freeze. I later learned that before my arrival, one bystander did roll him onto his back. That was exactly the wrong thing to do without securing his airway first.

If you ever have the misfortune of being the only hope someone has, wouldn't you desire being the best that you can be? Have a kit. Get some training. I hope and pray you never need to use it.

Jumper Cables

Many times, in my adult life, I have found myself in need of a pair of jumper cables. I have also used them to help others on several occasions. No vehicle should be without them. Buy the more expensive ones with heavy gauge wire.

Basic Tool Kit

A tool kit for your vehicle should enable you to tighten loose battery connections, replace a battery and replace damaged belts and hoses. It's also a good idea to carry replacement belts, hoses and wipers for your vehicle if you have the storage capacity to do so. The tool kit should also include tire plugs and a way to inflate a tire.

A Good Jack

The jacks that come with most vehicles are junk. A High Lift jack is probably the best but they're not for everyone. They can also hurt you if you're not trained to use them. In addition to the jack that came with my vehicle, I also carry a floor jack and a bottle jack. Do some research and upgrade to what is appropriate for your lifestyle and location.

Four-way Lug Wrench

Just as the jack that comes with modern vehicles is lacking, so is the included lug wrench. A proper four-way lug wrench will outperform them every time. It allows a smaller person to stomp on the end of the T if they lack the physical strength to break the lug nuts loose. Additionally, the perpendicular path of the handle provides far more leverage. It also gives you four different size sockets. It may not be your car that has a flat, you may be helping others with a different model vehicle. Without a lug wrench, the jack is useless. Get a proper one.

Extra Spare Tire

This may sound like overkill, but I really do carry two spare tires. Why? My reasoning is that sometimes it's not safe to stop when you have a flat (think civil unrest). If I had to drive on the flat tire long enough, a second one could blow. I once swerved to avoid an object in the road, but I could only swerve enough to get the driver's side tires clear. As for the tires on the passenger side, they both went flat. It happens.

I know carrying an additional spare isn't an option for everyone. I just want you to consider how you would handle a situation in which you have more than one flat tire. I have an SUV with a roof rack so it's easy for me to carry an extra spare tire.

A *Current* Road Atlas

Most folks these days typically navigate by means of a smartphone. I am no different. They are handy and convenient. However, electronics can fail, usually when you most need them. For this reason, I carry a *current* road atlas along with more detailed maps of the areas I frequent more often than others. A paper map doesn't require charging or satellite signal; have one!

Books

Boredom can be quite deadly to the overall morale of the human creature. Speaking for myself, a book is the answer. It's easy to become lost in a good book; before you know it, hours have passed. This is one of the strategies that inmates use to psychologically cope with incarceration, because it works. I generally keep a couple of books in my vehicle. My current ride-alongs are *Meditations* by Marcus Aurellius and the works of Emerson. Don't forget the kiddos; have a few books that are age appropriate for them and be sure they are thick enough to last a while. Drawing paper and pencils or even coloring books may buy you a few moments of peace and quiet with younger kids. Maybe.

Snow Chains

I keep a set of snow chains stuffed under one of the seats in my vehicle year-round. I can't drive very fast with them but at least I'll be moving. Even in situations other than snow, they can be used to turn a stuck vehicle into an unstuck one.

Backpack

A backpack, Bugout Bag, Get out of Dodge Bag, Go Bag, Bail Out Bag, Jump bag or whatever you want to call it, and whatever it is to you, should be kept in your vehicle. Think of it as an escape pod.

When travel by vehicle is no longer possible or optimal, you need a pack that can carry what you need to carry for as long as you need to carry it. The items inside are totally dependent upon the variables of each unique situation. There is no perfect list. Be sure you have footwear that is appropriate for the task at hand. They must be broken in *before* you actually need them. Blisters can reduce a 6'6" 250-pound man to a crumpled, useless mess. Trust me on this one. And remember, you must be fit enough to carry that bag. Fitness matters.

Medications/Special Needs

I am fortunate in that I am currently not dependent upon any medications. If you are not as fortunate, please be sure to have your prescriptions issued in the largest quantity possible; 90 days is a good goal. Be sure to have them with you! Your inhaler or blood pressure tablets will do you no good left at home. Keep the appropriate amounts on hand for your situation.

Take a moment to consider each person you may need to care for. If Grand Pappy Jack can't walk anymore, you should get comfortable with the idea of pushing him to safety in a wheelchair. Maybe you'll get a mountain bike with a trailer and transport him that way. Maybe if the situation is bad enough, you may say, "Hate your luck, Pappy; me and the kids gotta pop smoke. It's been real; thanks for the memories!" (Just kidding; I'd find a way to transport Pappy.)

If you have small children with you, that's going to be interesting. They leak from both ends and they do not come with an instruction manual. Furthermore, they each have a unique personality that must be considered when preparing to care for them.

In the case of an infant, it would be wise to have deep reserves of formula if that's what they feed on. Clean water to prepare the formula goes without saying. The bottles and nipples must be cleaned as well, so provide for that. These tiny creatures must be kept warm and dry. Diapers and baby wipes are a must; you should pack more than you can ever conceive of actually using, then pack some more. I pity the one that runs out of those little gems. Throw in some earplugs and mood stabilizing herbs for the rest of the crew and you're all set!

Conclusion

Your vehicle is your closest resupply point. Sometimes, you may catch a ride in someone else's vehicle. In such cases, you should grab your pack at a minimum. Maybe you should grab some water too. I think if most people took an honest look at their vehicle and asked themselves, "Am I ready for X to happen now?" The answer will usually be no. Never allow yourself to be stuck in the snowstorm equipped only with breath mints!

12 - Intelligence, Get Some

WHY DO WE NEED INTELLIGENCE?[2]
We need intelligence because everyone has blind spots.

Think of intelligence gathering and analysis as the keys to maintaining situational awareness. It's imperative that we understand what's happening beyond our line of sight.

One of my favorite quotes comes from Jack Welch, the former chief executive officer of General Electric, who said, "If the rate of change on the outside exceeds the rate of change on the inside, the end is near."

He was speaking about how businesses have to be ahead of changing business conditions and consumer demands, but the quote is just as applicable to us in emergency or survival conditions.

In a survival situation, there will be threats. We need to know about them before they become *our* problem.

If political, social, economic, or environmental conditions are deteriorating during an emergency, then we have to be able to monitor those conditions and determine how they'll affect us in the future.

What intelligence brings to the table is real-time situational awareness for real-time decision-making. It may even allow us to anticipate the future and better prepare for it.

---

2 Samuel Culper is a former Intelligence NCO and contractor. With over a decade of intelligence experience on three continents, including three years deployed to Iraq and Afghanistan, he's now the CEO of Forward Observer, an intelligence services company specializing in risk intelligence and conflict monitoring. Samuel is also the principal for the Fox Intelligence Group, an intelligence training company.

Ultimately, it gives us the ability to make well-informed, time-sensitive decisions in potentially life-or-death situations.

At the heart of intelligence is the ability to reduce uncertainty. If you're concerned about grid-down or financial collapse or the Golden Horde or some other event or threat, then some basic intelligence work should be at the top of your To Do list.

The OODA Loop

Colonel John Boyd, an Air Force fighter pilot, was the first to describe the decision-making process he called the OODA Loop. Because fighter pilots have to make split-second decisions, their ability to *Observe* a development, *Orient* to what that means, *Decide* which course of action they should take and then *Act* on it, is a critical part of their survivability in combat. Similarly, lots of tactical shooting trainers have incorporated the OODA Loop into their curriculum for the exact same reason.

That ability to Observe and Orient is the informational phase of the decision-making process. Can you imagine getting into a gunfight if you can't see or hear your opponent? Yet that's exactly what many are preparing to do on a larger level. We're limited by our field of vision and line of sight, but with an intelligence effort, we can begin to see things others don't.

What intelligence allows us to do during a survival scenario is not just see our threats or opponents, but potentially observe them before a conflict arises. This is called Early Warning, and it's one of the two key responsibilities of our intelligence element.

The second major responsibility is producing Threat Intelligence. Knowing that a gang is active in your area is a good first step. But we need to move beyond our intuitive approach to information and start using a structured, methodical process to completely remove our blind spots. In essence, we need to graduate from basic information and start producing intelligence.

The difference between information and intelligence is simple:

information is raw data. It hasn't been evaluated for value, nor have we determined its veracity. Intelligence, on the other hand, is the evaluated, assessed, and synthesized information that answers, "So what?" Hearing that there was a murder in your community is not intelligence; it's just information.

Identifying the perpetrator and his current location, finding out where and why the murder took place, determining how it's going to affect the community, and compiling it into a consumable product is intelligence.

In any survival situation, we're going to face one of two problems: either we're not going to have enough information to make well-informed, time-sensitive decisions or we're going to have too much information to wade through, which will slow down our decision-making process. So, what's the lesson? We need to begin developing streams of information now in order to avoid problem number one, and we need to know what to do with that information in order to avoid problem number two. Let's focus on solving problem number one for now.

It seems like a poor decision to believe that we'll have access to lots of information during an SHTF scenario. I'm more than willing to concede that information will not be as cheap and easy to collect then as it is now. So, the more information we can collect now, the less we'll have to collect later. For now—while information is cheap and easy—we're going to focus mainly on the internet and other widely available sources of information.

Cheap and easy information

Say what you want about Google, but there is no better online tool to collect massive amounts of information. (And that obviously goes both ways, as it's always collecting information about you, so it's a good idea to use online anonymity tools and an anonymous or pseudonymous email address.) We run into a problem, however, when the requirement to collect information online monopolizes our time.

Who has time to sit at a desk and search online for hours on end for information that may not even exist? Not me, and that's why we need to automate collection as much as possible.

Google Alerts is a great resource for automated intelligence collection.

Some of my searches include:

- "Waller County" and "Texas" and "crime"
- "Waller County" and "Texas" and "drug"
- "Waller County" and "Texas" and "gang"
- "Waller County" and "Texas" and "corruption"
- "Waller County" and "Texas" and "violence"
- "Waller County" and "Texas" and "Sheriff "
- "Waller County" and "Texas" and "whatever else is relevant to your security"

Be sure to replace "Waller County" with your town and start getting more local information. You could even do searches for the name of your community or subdivision, or for nearby landmarks.

What Google Alerts does for us is creates a daily roll-up of new articles that Google finds about those subjects. I start my day every morning checking my Google Alerts to find more information about my area, and it saves me a great deal of time. Now, assuming that our searches use quality logic, one problem we may run into is a lack of reporting, especially if you live in a very rural area. And if that's the case, then we have a few options. First, I'd encourage you to go volunteer with your county sheriff 's office or local police department and get to know the crime, drug, and gang information from knowledgeable sources.

Second, we could approach our local paper, if they're not already doing it, to start writing more about crime or drugs or gangs (or all three) in the area.

Third, if there's no area paper or they're not interested, then we could start doing it ourselves. (Local area "micro-papers" are a great way to get our message out to the community, as well.)

I'd also encourage you to search Twitter and other social media for your area. For instance, a search for Hempstead, Texas on Twitter doesn't seem to reveal much pertinent information immediately, however, I'm identifying people who live nearby posting about what's important to them, and that's certainly of some intelligence value. After a little digging, I found a like-minded individual and discovered information about a group that could pose a threat to my community. Just knowing that the group exists is a great start to becoming more secure.

If you're concerned about critical infrastructure in the area, I'd steer you towards the Energy Information Administration (EIA) and their U.S. Energy Mapping System, where you can see the critical infrastructure in your county (or across the country). If you're interested in the human terrain, sites like City Data (city-data.com) are great resources with tons of relevant information and mapping tools.

And, of course, we can't forget about the radio networks. You can rely on your ham radio guy, or you can study for the technician or general class amateur radio test and begin learning ham radio yourself. Forget about transmitting for a moment ... our ability to listen into communications—whether they're from first responders, law enforcement, or a ham radio operator passing along relevant information—is a mission-critical skill for the intelligence element. If we don't have around-the-clock monitoring of at least a police scanner, then we're missing out on potentially a lot of important information.

More difficult collection options

In a grid-down situation, or a scenario where our intelligence requirement can't be satisfied with open source information, we're going to rely heavily on other humans to collect for us. Let's steer clear of calling this "source operations" because it doesn't need to be that complex or professional to get us through an emergency.

By expanding our circle of friends and acquaintances, we're expanding our access to information. Building rapport and becoming friends with individuals who are likely to have important information is going to greatly increase our ability to maintain situational awareness.

Beyond that, we should be using the eyes and ears of those in our community. We need to get our neighbors "bought in" to the idea that community security is everyone's responsibility. I hate to use the phrase "See Something, Say Something", however, DHS is on track to building lots of channels of information of potential intelligence value. Our message to the community could be as simple as, "Let me know if you see anything suspicious."

Alternatively, starting (or joining) a neighborhood watch program is a great option. Not only will we get access to law enforcement officers and crime information, but we can also build a reporting system and give our community members a seat at the table. It also gives us a great excuse (something we call "cover for action") to go door-to-door asking questions and providing information as the block leader of the Neighborhood Watch.

Finally, we absolutely need to be using police scanners and any other technology we have in order to stay on top of the changing security situation. I highly recommend the Uniden Home Patrol II police scanner.

Grid Down Intelligence Gathering

First things first, we have to get eyes on the surrounding area and/or the neighborhood. In a worst-case crisis scenario, that typically means getting an elevated vantage point, being in a forward position to look for threats, or setting up a listening post/observation post (LP/OP). The last thing we want to do in intelligence is to be surprised. And since 'finding, knowing, and never losing' the threat is our job, that means that we have to be proactive.

The most immediate threats are going to have the greatest proximity, so the quickest way to identify potential threats is to get them in our view before we're in theirs.

Simultaneously, we need to power up our police scanner(s) and radio(s). Our police scanners already need to be programmed for our area. I'd set someone at a desk with earphones plugged into the scanner. During a crisis scenario, we should have 24/7 coverage on the police scanner. If we're going to get consistent, authoritative intelligence information about events in the area, it's most likely to originate from emergency services.

Next, I also recommend putting someone on another radio, such as a ham radio, to search out transmissions on radio frequencies that our police scanner won't pick up. This could be a goldmine of information, especially if we can listen into a conversation. Be sure to log the times, frequencies and call signs of these communications.

If we can begin visually monitoring the area around our home, listening to the police scanner, and begin searching for frequencies in use around us, then we have a *really* good start on gathering information about what's going on around us.

The next thing I would do in my neighborhood is start contacting neighbors, door-to-door. My goal would be to get them to contact me if they see or hear anything; that way, if things got really bad, I've already established contact with them and can bring them on board for community security. I live in a pretty good neighborhood in a pretty safe area. Chances are good that most folks want to keep it that way, so I'm offering a solution to that problem. I expect most in my neighborhood will volunteer to help me because I've already built relationships with them.

Remember that every set of eyes and ears in your neighborhood is a sensor. I want to make sure that I can collect as much of what's seen and heard as possible. That means that I need to influence them or otherwise gain their cooperation to feed me information. As a former intelligence analyst, that's been an easy sell to my prepping neighbors. Should you be in a similar situation with neighbors already on the block, as a group, you should nominate a person to be in charge of collating information and building out the security picture.

We're now getting into the world of very basic Human Intelligence, called HUMINT. Plainly stated, that's gathering information from conversations with humans. That means getting out and talking to people.

With the internet, radios, and scanners, we can be very wide and very deep in our intelligence gathering. That's a 1:n ratio, which is often immediate and real-time. We have one collection platform, in this case, a radio receiver; and we can scan a very wide band to collect information from anyone who's transmitting. But when we deal with human intelligence, we're often on a 1:1 ratio; that is, one collector speaking to one source at any given time. That's a very slow and difficult way to do the business of intelligence gathering and underscores a real need for us to be out in our community getting to know folks before a grid-down event.

Instead of a typical 1:1, I want you to consider the scalability of that ratio. If one person is limited to gathering intelligence information from one person at a time, wouldn't it make sense to scale that ratio to 5 or 10, if at all possible? It absolutely would. Every set of eyes and ears is a sensor, so we, as an intelligence element tasked with providing intelligence for our security, should absolutely be interested in encouraging community members to passively collect lots of information. All that information is reported back to us, and then we're engaged in the arduous task of compiling and evaluating that information in order to create intelligence.

Intelligence doesn't produce itself, so it's incumbent on us to build that capability. The more accurate information we have, the better informed we can be. Without first being well-informed, making high-risk, time-sensitive decisions just got a whole lot more complicated.

Our goals during a crisis scenario should be producing *early warning* of threats, events, or changing conditions, and *threat intelligence to better understand them.*

Let's say that we identify some gang members in the area, or we identify the location of a police roadblock, or maybe we're tipped off about another threat in the area. We've received the information, it's been vetted, and we assess that the information is accurate. Before we alert members of the group, we need to figure out how we're going to spread the message. This is not a particularly difficult step, because we're so limited in our options during an emergency scenario.

How do we spread awareness and get community involvement? In a worst case SHTF scenario, I envision something like this for my community...

I go door to door around my neighborhood and check on my neighbors, many of whom I already know. I explain that I'm monitoring the emergency situation. I ask for help in keeping their eyes peeled. If they are very responsive, then I get them signed up for a proactive community watch, where they will help me monitor who's coming in and out of the neighborhood, as well as what's going on just outside that line of sight.

For everyone else, I will explain that we'll be working 24/7 to alert the neighborhood about what's going on. Doing this or having someone go around door to door for me, will allow us to gauge the neighborhood's attitudes and opinions about what's going on (not to mention identifying who's home and who's not). We call this 'atmospherics' and, as an intelligence analyst, it's vital for me to understand the mood of the community.

Now here comes the difficult part. In a grid-down or any other crisis situation, how do I push out intelligence to the community? Grid-down: by courier and word of mouth, most likely. Here are a number of ways that we can disseminate the early warning and/or threat intelligence to community members of like mind who agree to help provide security for the area. What follows are merely some suggestions...

1. **Town hall meetings**—As long as we have incoming information, one of my first steps for my neighborhood is to establish a daily town hall where community members are briefed on the day's new information. At least for my area, being proactive and building a sense of cooperation is part of my plan to

ensure that we all stay as calm as possible. The other part of this town hall includes eliciting feedback about those who will be in need. It's a great way for me to update my neighbors on what's going on, and in turn continue to gather information about developing situations in the community. Additionally, this provides me a great deal of legitimacy that I can use to ensure that we make good security decisions. The last thing I want is for the neighborhood to descend into a Mad-Max-esque sequel where poor decisions can exploit a sense of panic or unrest. That begins with building cooperation on a neighbor-to-neighbor basis.

2. **Radio nets**—We should already be linking up with ham radio operators in the area (and becoming ham radio operators our-selves—I recommend the Gordon West books on Technician Class and General Class ham licenses). This is not only going to be key in expanding my access to information, but this is also going to allow me to disseminate intelligence to my own area. Outside of high frequency ham radio, we have some other options, especially concerning low-power transmissions that would just cover the bubble of our immediate area. Trans-mitting on a predetermined VHF/UHF frequency would allow the neighborhood access to our scheduled updates. Another option is FM radio. By the letter of the law, I believe one must obtain a license to transmit on low-power AM/FM. Transmit-ting on a local FM frequency would be a great way to provide scheduled updates to the area, too. The time is now to link up with local radio operators who are like-minded and begin identifying solutions for your area. Get your local radio expert to weigh in on what's best for your area.

3. **Micro-newspapers**—The Appalachian Messenger was a great example of a micro-newspaper. It was started to compete with their local liberal paper and enjoyed great circulation for their area. This may not be a great solution for the average

community, but as long as we have the means, then we can churn out a onepager each week containing the weekly roll-up of information— an intelligence summary, if you will.

4. **Phone calls**—Yeah, I know—it puts you "on the grid", but there's no more efficient way of getting into contact with folks as long as cell towers are working. My first preference is to meet with community members face to face; however, I'd also like to attempt to call neighbors who aren't home and find out where they are. As one caveat: remember to never transmit sensitive information electronically, including via email or phone.

In conclusion, I just want to encourage everyone to consider information as a part of preparedness. We don't need to be James Bond or begin complex espionage operations, but we do need access to timely, relevant, accurate, specific, actionable, and predictive information.

Having all the food, water, firearms, and medical supplies in the world does you little good if you suffer what we call 'strategic shock' or being exploited by a threat that you didn't know existed.

Please learn about active and potential threats in your area. Intelligence reduces uncertainty, and I want to give my family and community every operational advantage over area threats. That includes domain awareness—the informational advantage over those threats. If we can remain better informed than they are, then we have a significant advantage.

13 - Frequencies, Flags, and Flares3

W E LIVE IN AN ERA of convenient mass communication. Everyone is attached to their cell phone in one way or another. It's a type of safety net in a lot of ways. We can get most of our information from them, our entertainment from them, and if we get into trouble, help is just a call away. And most of us will never stop to think about the huge infrastructure that supports it. What would happen if all that came crashing down? That dreaded sound of *"all circuits are busy"* or *"no service"* causes an uneasy feeling. How will I communicate if and when I need to? How will I know what's going on in the world? It's a tough question that always leads to radio. How else can you create an infrastructure that you 100% control? I don't know of any other real option. And even though it takes some work to get right, anyone can do it. We're going to break it down and cover how to create that infrastructure where there otherwise would be none.

No survival plan is complete without the ability to communicate and a way to listen. Whether it's for simply monitoring and maintaining reliable contact around your own retreat or networking over a region, understanding communications is as persistent a challenge to the prepper as is weapons craft, field craft, and basic sustainment. Although it's a skill usually either overlooked, oversimplified or simply

---

3   This chapter was written by our good friend NC Scout over at American Partisan. If you're looking for training in tactical comms, these are the guys to call. Not only are they great with tactical communications, they are also very well-rounded instructors in other skills. We highly recommend them for training. You can contact NC Scout through his website, www.americanpartisan.org

misunderstood, knowing the basics of a robust communications plan is a cornerstone of preparedness.

No group's plan is complete without a basic, local commo setup and by following the simple plan we'll cover, reliable communications are definitely within your reach.

Categories of Radio Services

Let's talk a bit about the three broad categories of personal radio: *License Free, Trust Licensed,* and *Amateur Radio* (also known as Ham Radio). Each has its own strengths and weaknesses. License-free communications include *Citizen's Band (CB), Multi-Use Radio Service (MURS) and Family Radio Service (FRS). General Mobile Radio Service (GMRS)* is shared with FRS and is licensed through a trust covering an entire group. And finally, we have the broadest category, *Amateur Radio*, which offers the absolute most options and nearly unlimited capability.

CB: The Grandaddy

The first type folks should look at is *Citizen's Band* (or CB) radios. CB, while definitely old school, is a low power and extremely common means of radio communication. There's no license requirement and they're found in pretty much every corner of the US. And while using one makes me think about the good ole days of the Dukes of Hazard, CB is still used in many rural places as a robust alternative to phones. It's the old school survival prepper radio, and it's still very much a viable option. You can find them in any truck stop and usually most flea markets and keeping a setup in your truck or bugout vehicle is a no-brainer.

CB is an interesting animal; and in the US, it is standardized into 40 channels:

CB 1: 26.965	CB11: 27.085	CB21: 27.215	CB31: 27.315
CB 2: 26.975	CB12: 27.105	CB22: 27.225	CB32: 27.325
CB 3: 26.985	CB13: 27.115	CB23: 27.235	CB33: 27.335
CB 4: 27.005	CB14: 27.125	CB24: 27.255	CB34: 27.345
CB 5: 27.015	CB15: 27.135	CB25: 27.245	CB35: 27.355
CB 6: 27.025	CB16: 27.155	CB26: 27.265	CB36: 27.365
CB 7: 27.035	CB17: 27.165	CB27: 27.275	CB37: 27.375
CB 8: 27.055	CB18: 27.175	CB28: 27.285	CB38: 27.385
CB 9: 27.065	CB19: 27.185	CB29: 27.295	CB39: 27.395
CB10: 27.075	CB20: 27.205	CB30: 27.305	CB40: 27.405

Channel 9 is typically reserved for emergencies and *Channel 19* is used as a common calling channel. These days you'll find most of the action on CB around those two channels and on 6, which is where pirates running a high amount of power talk over long distances, called *shooting the skip*.

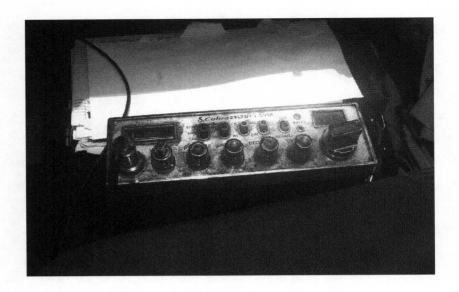

This is illegal in most places, but still good to know as a source of info if the world goes sideways. Channel 19 is great for listening to while driving on the interstates just for the information on traffic conditions and where the cops are sitting. These are kind of the general rules, and in each corner of the US your results may vary. For example, around where I live, many of the channels are used by migrant labor to communicate off grid. *No phone, no problem*, and if you happen to se habla espanol, you can score a heck of deal on laying hens and cowboy boots. They use it because it's so common, and it's likely that those old CBs will still be running long after the rest of the world goes quiet. Simple to install and even easier to use, there's no reason not to have one.

MURS: The Rural Option

Multi Use Radio Service, or MURS, is five channels in the VHF band from 151-154mHz, making it a very good option for folks living in rural areas. VHF typically performs better in rural areas. Most often, you'll find MURS being used for driveway alarm systems and motion detectors, made by a company called Dakota Alert. I use these for rural security, setting one frequency to each detector so that I know immediately which routes are covered.

- MURS 1 : 151.820
- MURS 2 : 151.880
- MURS 3 : 151.94
- MURS 4 : 154.57
- MURS 5 : 154.600

But because MURS performs fairly well where I live, it's a great option for community networking as well. Since it's only five channels, it's a bit easier for folks new to radio to wrap their heads around and eliminates a lot of confusion. Since it's still relatively unknown even after being around for nearly twenty years, don't expect a lot of people to be talking in your area. In fact, if you do happen to find a MURS net local to you, those are people that you need to know. Because of these reasons, I tend to fall back on it first when other options have failed.

FRS/GMRS: The Most Common Choice

 Family Radio Service, or FRS and General Mobile Radio Service, or GMRS are two versions of the spread of space in the UHF band from 462mHz to 468mHz. FRS is license free and GMRS requires a license that covers an entire trust of the licensee. Confused yet? FRS is restricted by power output, limited to 2 watts legally. GMRS, on the other hand, allows you to pump out up to 50 watts as well as use a repeater system for everyone on your trust.

UHF tends to perform better in urban areas, and the radios themselves that most will likely have are the very simple Motorolas that claim to have insane ranges. *They don't.* Realistically you'll get a half mile or so, and that's about it. I'm not a huge fan of FRS in particular because even though it's popular for hunting clubs around where I live, it's extremely common and offers no security. If everyone is on it, then it will turn into a mess in the event of an emergencysomething we definitely don't want.

1: 462.5625	12: 467.6625
2: 462.5875	13: 467.6875
3: 462.6125	14: 467.7125
4: 462.6375	15: 462.5500
5: 462.6625	16: 462.5750
6: 462.6875	17: 462.6000
7: 462.7125	18: 462.6250
8: 467.5625	19: 462.6500
9: 467.5875	20: 462.6750
10: 467.6125	21: 462.7000
11: 467.6375	22: 462.7250

But that said, they do work, and they are simple for the less technically oriented, which has a value all its own. If you're trying to stand up a local communications network in an area and that's all you've got, then you're not necessarily under-gunned, but you definitely need to know that there's next to no security with it.

Ham Radio: The Best Option

Amateur Radio, nicknamed *'Ham'* after the *'ham-fisted operators'* tapping out Morse code, is the broadest and best option anyone into survival communications has. With Ham radio, you're tapping into a world of nearly unlimited resources and the biggest network of people actively using radios. I know of no other way to effectively communicate over regions with the vast number of methods and modes available to the end user. If you want to do it and understand the basics, you can do it.

Ham radio requires a license and they come in three levels: *Technician, General* and *Amateur Extra*. A Tech license gets you on the air on the VHF and UHF bands, while General allows you to also use most of HF, and Amateur Extra opens them all up. The licensing fee is usually $15 and the license itself is free, lasting for 10 years and free to renew. For each, you take a multiple-choice test that you can practice online, and the questions range from basic operating skills to more technical oriented questions. It's all pretty straightforward and it gets you into the real world of communications capability, which is where you want to be.

My amateur radio station, capable of communicating on all bands and in all modes, licensed and unlicensed, covering everything from my local network to everywhere in the world.

But one thing to note is that most people, once they get that ham ticket, tend to forget about the license-free options. I look at them all as tools in the same toolbox, and I like having the most options on the table, and you should too. When one option may not work for local needs, another one will. And when I need a regional or even global communications, I've got that too. It's all about having the most capability.

US Amateur Radio Frequency Range:

160m:	1.8-2mHz
80m:	3.5-4mHz
60m:	(1)5.332mHz, (2)5.348, (3)5.3585, (4)5.373, (5)5.405
40m:	7-7.3mHz
30m:	10.1-10.150mHz CW/DATA ONLY
20m:	14-14.350mHz
17m:	18.068-18.168mHz
15m:	21-21.450mHz
12m:	24.890-24.990mHz
10m:	28-29.7mHz
6m:	50-54mHz
2m:	144-148mHz
1.25m:	222-225mHz
70cm:	420-450mHz
33cm:	902-928mHz
23cm:	1270-1295mHz

Starting Out—A Few Words About Gear

Normally, everyone just starting out focuses on what to buy. People usually pick up a couple radios and hope they work; after all, the box said it would. Sometimes they do, sometimes they don't. And when they don't, at least in my experience, it's not the fault of the equipment but more likely operator error. *You gotta know what you have on hand and how to best use it.* And that means knowing its weaknesses and strengths, which you really only know by using them in the real world. I run my own choices of equipment daily and put them to the test regularly, so I know exactly what they're capable of and have no unrealistic expectations for what they aren't. For most people, those first few radios should be super common and very inexpensive. *The simpler, the better.* That way, we can lay a foundation, and as your skills grow, so should your gear. But it won't do you any good, and maybe even end up badly, if you buy the most expensive, over-complicated stuff out there and then never learn how to use it.

Dual Band HTs

Normally, the first radio most preppers & survivalists will come across is one of the very inexpensive *Dual Band Handheld* radios (*handi-talkies*, or *HTs*) commonly found online for $20-25. I call these CCRs (Cheap Chinese Radios), with the most common version being the Baofeng UV-5R. They're very simple and the startup time is low, with the batteries and antenna built into the package. There are some frequencies you'll definitely want to avoid transmitting on, such as analog public service and Marine band; but if you know what you're doing, you can have quite a bit of capability in a cheap package. What

Two HTs on my
patrolling kit.

(L-R) Quansheng UV-R50, Baofeng UV-5R

"dual band" means is that the radios transmit on VHF and UHF frequencies, which is a big asset.

Are there better radios on the market? For sure. But the UV-5R offers a whole lot for the money, including decent transmitting power, a decent receiver and a very long battery life. For what they are, I still can't find a reason not to own a handful of them. And not only that, these days it's the radio most folks will have. Quantity, so the saying goes, is a quality all its own. You can program them either by hand (a tedious process) or with a free program called Chirp, loading all of the license-free channels such as *Multi-Use Radio Service* (*MURS*) and *Family Radio Service* (*FRS*) for transmitting and monitoring the NOAA weather frequencies, Marine radio, and if you have an Amateur Radio or *General Mobile Radio Service* (*GMRS*) license, you can transmit on those as well. But not only that, it includes an FM broadcast radio, which comes in handy.

Yaesu VX-6R.

Stepping up in quality, I suggest also picking up a Yaesu VX-6R and getting what's known as a MARS/CAP mod done to the radio. This mod unlocks the full-transmit range; they come stock-only, having the amateur radio bands unlocked. These radios are waterproof, shockproof, and receive everything from the AM broadcast band to shortwave, aircraft, amateur, and all of the license-free stuff, so it's a heck of a lot of capability in a handheld package. I strongly suggest having a couple of them per group just for the receiver quality alone.

QYT-8900 mobile radio. Compact and powerful.

At this point, you're probably wondering why I haven't said anything about the little Motorola handhelds you can pick up in Walmart. I don't suggest having them; for what they cost, you're further ahead with a Dual Band HT, which puts out more power but more importantly, allows us to use external antennas. And while yeah, that's technically not legal on FRS, when the chips are down, I highly doubt anyone will be coming out of the woodwork to tell you to stop.

Mobile and Base Station Radios

After HTs, the next type of radio you should pick up is a mobile. These are the larger radios you'll find in trucks or more permanent setups. While it takes a little more knowledge to get a mobile radio up and running, it's not all that hard and provides your retreat with a higher-powered unit. Mobiles and base stations normally push out anywhere from 10 to 100 watts, allowing for much more coverage than what you'll get with a handheld. Coupled with a higher and more efficient antenna, a mobile will reach much further, allowing you to talk to the more distant retreats in your area.

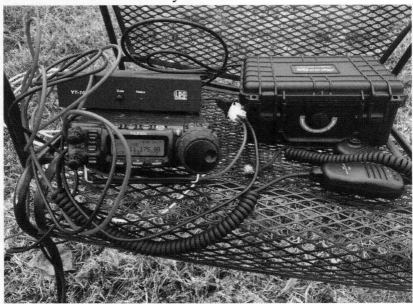

Yaesu FT-857 with LDG tuner. Its small size makes it portable for use just about anywhere.

Like with that UV-5R, there's also a low-cost mobile unit that works pretty well. The QYT KT-8900 is a durable little radio that has lasted over the past few years I've had it and it's been run through both hot and humid summers and very cold winters out in the field, never failing me yet. Costing under $100, it's a great starter radio for any prepper's retreat and has the same basic features as the UV-5R while putting out 25 watts of power. What you need to get up and running is a good antenna, just an aluminum VHF/UHF J-Pole and decent quality coax cable. I grab my coax from truck stops; the CB coax they sell works just fine. Get that antenna put up on a mast and you're all set.

Stepping up to HF, there are two radios I suggest having. The first is the *Yaesu FT-857*. It's a bit older but it offers everything in one package—HF, VHF, and UHF, all in one unit. This is the radio that you'd want in a central location of your retreat, being able to communicate both locally, regionally and even globally. Because it's pretty small, you can fit it nearly anywhere and it pumps out up to 100 watts. Every retreat's commo plan should include one.

Keep in mind, you'll also need a tuner. A tuner is a device that 'tunes' an HF antenna to the correct electrical match, making sure that you don't burn your radio up while transmitting when using the very long antennas that you have on HF. A tuner is a must-have; think of it as an insurance plan for your HF radio. I prefer LDG, but there are a few brands out there that make good tuners. LDG is just the one I've had the best experiences with.

The excellent Com-mRadio CTX-10, pictured here with a Quansheng TG-UV2. Together, they've got most of a small group's communications needs covered while remaining off the grid.

The second radio I strongly suggest having is a low-powered HF radio, also known as a QRP rig. These normally put out between 5 and 10 watts. The reason I suggest them is that when compared to their higher-powered versions, they consume less power, both when transmitting and while monitoring, so they won't eat through your batteries as fast. On top of that, the best QRP radios on the market today, the Elecraft KX-2 & 3, and the CommRadio CTX-10, have built-in tuners and batteries which keep your equipment simple and robust if you're operating from a backpack—like I would if I sent out a small patrol for several days that planned on traveling outside my region.

A quick word about Field Phones

The last piece of equipment you should consider having in a retreat is a good set of field phones. They're best used for static positions around a retreat, such as a guard position or to network houses around a larger compound. I use a few sets of TA-312s, which were standard US military field phones until the 1980s and still used among special operations forces even today. With two phones linked by wire, it's as secure as a communications system can be. On top of that, they're

(L-R) Czech surplus field phone connected to TA-312 field phone. They work well with one another. Simple, robust, reliable.

about as robust as a Kalashnikov and don't need much in terms of supportjust a couple of D-cell batteries and some twin lead wire, and you're good to go.

Wait, what kind of wire? In the Army, we used what was called WD-1 wire, which was nothing more than lightweight aluminum core double wire. You can get them in giant spools, but it can get on the expensive side. Other options work fine; I've used everything from lamp cord to claymore wire, and as long as you have a hot wire and a cold wire, you're good to go.

I use those 312s because it's what I have, but you might be asking if some of the other field phones on the market can work. They do. We've used European WW2 to Cold War era surplus phones with my 312s, and they work just fine. So, if you find yourself in a situation with several different models of surplus phones, as long as you've got a hot and cold wire, the phones will work.

Powering Your Radios Off Grid

With your basic equipment needs met, now we need to talk about powering all of this stuff. None of it does us any good if we don't have a way to keep the juice flowing, and that begins and ends with deep cycle batteries. What I suggest is the older *Sealed Lead Acid Batteries (SLA)* which you can find in any farm supply store to power electric fences. While there are newer, lighter, and better batteries for off-grid use on the market such as *Lithium Iron Phosphate (LiFePO4)*,

A 35 Amp hour sealed lead acid battery with a homemade Anderson Power Pole cable. Inexpensive, easy to charge, and will power your station for a long- time off grid.

Mil-Spec 30-Watt backpack solar panel made by Global Star.

I'm fairly old school when it comes to batteries; I know what works and I don't stray too far from proven technology. SLAs are cheap, last forever, and work in wide environments ranging from hot, humid and wet conditions to very cold and very dry. And while the LiFePO4s are far more lightweight, they're expensive and harder to find. But whatever you run, just keep in mind your mobile radios are almost always 12-volt *Direct Current* (*DC*), and usually have a power tolerance of 11-13.8 volts.

Keeping those batteries charged off grid might present another challenge, but what I'll suggest is investing in several solar panel arrays to keep them topped off. Solar might seem intimidating at first but charging SLAs from a panel is actually pretty simple. A basic setup can be picked up for a couple hundred bucks at any Harbor Freight or similar hardware store, and the startup time is almost zero. These days, many of the packages are ready to roll right out of the box, and as long as you've got a charge controller and the right connectors, you're good to go.

Speaking of connectors, I strongly recommend standardizing on

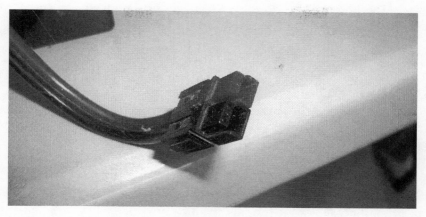

Anderson Power Pole connectors make all of your communications power connections simple and robust.

Anderson Power Poles. They're a very simple way of making every connection in your equipment arsenal the exact same. The way they work is by crimping on a connector to a standard power cord then snapping the plastic housing in place. Something I like to do is solder the crimps and, for added strength, melt a piece of shrink tubing to the joint; that way, the crimps can't back out. I rig the power cables to every one of my radios like this so that I can use any power source that I also have a plug rigged for. And in case I don't have the proper connector for any given battery, I have a cable with battery clamps on one end and Anderson Power Poles on the other, so that I can use any 12v power source I might come across.

Putting It All Together: Creating A Competent Communications Plan

Local, Local, Local

Now that we've talked about the gear, we need to focus on our retreat or our group's needs. The first place to begin with any plan is to work on our own local network. Map out where they are in relation to you. The best way to do that is to pull out a map of your area, any type of map, and mark where your places are. Figure out how much distance is between the points. Then ask yourself some questions:

1. How big is our own retreat?
2. How much distance might we have to cover to other retreats?
3. What is our terrain like?

If the answer to the first two is smaller than an average sized county, the good news is that creating a quick and dirty radio network is pretty simple. If other retreats in our network of like-minded folks are in our general area, maybe in the neighboring county, we can still make things happen with relative ease. It's when we need to cover longer distances that we'll run into some problemsbut let's dial it back to local coverage.

What's needed is known as *Line Of Sight* (*LOS*) communications. These are your VHF and UHF bands, with VHF working better in rural conditions and UHF favoring urban environments. Generally speaking, these radio waves travel out to the horizon; *if you can see it, you can communicate with it*. The way that we do this is by having our handhelds with the folks out doing thingsworking around the retreat, a patrol in town, whateverand the mobile unit back at the retreat's *Command Post* (*CP*). That way, the most powerful radio is at the center of the coverage area and with it; and it has the best antenna placed on a mast, giving us that longer line of sight over the short, stubby antennas on a handheld.

So, I brought up that question of range. With LOS communications, there are two ways to resolve getting a broader range. The higher the antenna, the further the line of sight. The more power, the further the line of sight. And if you combine the two, you'll get a lot more range than you would separately. In addition, the better that one antenna will receive all the other signals in the same coverage area; so even if they have a weaker signal, you'll be able to pull them in. So, what that means for the layman is that the better the coverage you've built

at your CP, the better the radios inside your network are also going to perform. Get that main antenna up high, and you'll have better results.

What role does terrain play? Quite a bitit's important to know that if you're in a rural area versus an urban area to get an idea of what works best for where you are. But on top of that, it's also a good idea to have the flexibility to go between both VHF and UHF, just in case one doesn't work but the other does. But let's go back to LOS theory; if there's a mountain for example, that you can't see over, then communicating to the other side is going to be trouble. But if you're standing on that mountain, now your line of sight is much further than it was at the basemeaning you can communicate much further than you would have otherwise.

Regional Coverage

The next logical step is building regional coverage. The way we do that is with Beyond Line of Sight radio, which uses the High Frequency, or HF radio bands. HF relies on what's known as skywave propagation to bounce signals off of the different layers of the ionosphere. The ionosphere is made of multiple layers that are energized in different ways by the sun. This is sometimes called 'shooting the skip', and it allows us to send a signal over an entire region or even worldwide.

There's a lot of use in having HF coverage even if you have no plans on transmitting. Here, you'll find shortwave broadcasts that are most commonly official news outlets of many nations; and while it might be propaganda in some cases, in a SHTF world, it comes in handy getting information from places other than the mainstream US media. Typically, shortwave is better at night, but many stations can still be heard during the morning and even into the afternoons in some regions. It just depends on where you are.

HF coverage is from 3-30Mhz, and is typically broken down into different bands that are named for the wavelength they're measured in. Each performs slightly different, but the most useful bands for the survivalist or prepper are the 20 meter band, or 14mHz, for global communication, the 40m band, or 7mHz for regional coverage during the day, and 80m, or 3.5mHz for regional coverage at night. It's on these bands that you're going to find the most useful traffic, and many groups hold weekly preparedness nets on the air. But it's also great for sharing regional information that you'd otherwise have a hard time sending, giving real-time status updates on the conditions in your area.

Near Vertical Incidence Skywave

Near Vertical Incidence Skywave, or *NVIS*, is a way to propagate those same HF signals while eliminating the skip zones. The way we do this is by taking the same antenna that we use for HF and bringing it close to the groundthat way our signal bounces straight up and comes straight back down, eliminating any of the skip zones we'd have otherwise. NVIS is a really good option if you're living in a mountainous area where your line of sight would otherwise be very limited. But it is also nearly bulletproof in its ability to network retreats over a region.

The basic rule of thumb with NVIS is that you want to use 40m during the day and 80m at night. Since both of these reflect from the F layer, and the F layer changes properties when ionized by the sun, they perform differently at different times of the day. I've found that 80m works well even in the early morning and early afternoon hours, with 40m working best during the middle of the day.

Creating a Simple, Bulletproof Plan

All of the equipment in the world won't do us any good if we don't at least have some sort of plan. I use what we call a *PACE Plan*, which stands for *Primary, Alternate, Contingency*, and *Emergency*. This creates four layers to our communications plan, so that no matter what, we've got another option. Primary and Alternate should be basically interchangeable. For building a tactical PACE Plan as part of a larger *Signals Operating Instructions* (*SOI*), I suggest having the two on opposite bands; if one is VHF, the other should be UHF—that way if one magically stops working, maybe the other band will work. But on the tactical side of things, it also mitigates an opponent's ability to monitor you if you're all of a sudden moving to another frequency several hundred megahertz away.

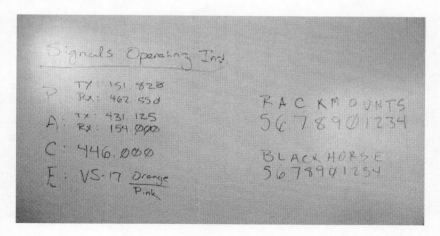

PACE Plan written out on the whiteboard in my Tactical Operations Center (TOC).

The Contingency frequency is the backup. If the Primary and Alternate have both failed, the Contingency frequency is used for linking up with friendly forces. This should be constantly monitored in your CP, with one radio switched to it and monitoring it at all times while a patrol is out. It should only be used for calling either the team that's in trouble or calling the team that's in charge of recovering them; that way, the actual radio chatter is kept to a minimum.

The final layer in the PACE Plan is Emergency and should be non-electronic. Since it's the last line of defense, it's got to work no matter what; and to keep Murphy from meddling in our plans as much as possible, no batteries should be involved. For the Emergency line, I typically use a blaze orange panel called a VS-17 as well as a signal mirror; but for each group, it's up to you. It could be anything from signal flares to colored smoke. Just make sure everyone knows the emergency signal for going out and the return/response signal before heading out.

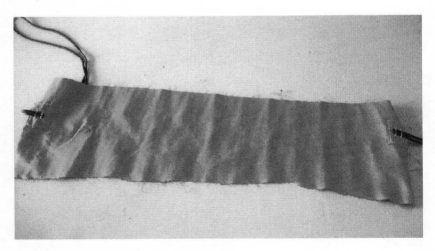

VS-17 panel.

Summing it up

A strong understanding of your communications needs will go a long way to building a bulletproof plan. Once you know what you need, you can quickly come up with a plan for training and equipping your group. But the biggest thing to remember about it is that it's not magic; communications requires constant practice, just like basic rifle marksmanship, daily PT, land navigation and every other skill. You've got to keep them sharp.

I don't believe in having the 'designated commo guy' just like I don't believe in having the 'designated medical guy' or 'designated weapons guy'. Everyone on the team needs to have a basic understanding of the core concepts, because the reality is the 'designated' guy for that skill may not always be there. It's the team's responsibility to be as knowledgeable on as many tasks as possibleand while we all have our fortes, a group should include as much training in communications as they do everything else. Your life might just depend on it.

Shoot, Move, Communicate

14 - I'm Hurt, Now What?

Medicine, the only profession that labours inces-
santly to destroy the reason for its own existence.
—James Brice

I N THE HIGHLY ADVANCED WORLD we live in today, advance-
ments in medical technology and the study of disease and viruses
at the genetic level have increased life expectancy dramatically.
According to Our World Data (https://ourworldindata.org/life-ex-
pectancy), the average life expectancy was just 39.4 years of age in
1950. Contrast that with the 78.9 years observed in 2015 and we can
see we've nearly doubled the number of years we get to enjoy on this
planet.

Several things have allowed us to live longer lives. The aforementioned advances in the medical field for certain, but others have as well,
from sanitary sewers and running water to technology taking a lot of
the physical burden from our daily lives. This also has the effect of
lowering our life expectancy at the same time through lack of exercise
and a sedentary lifestyle.

In the world we foresee in the not too distant future, this last point
will become moot. Everyone will once again become active. For
many, this will bring about unintended consequences, both good and
bad. America will lose its spare tire. Everyone will lose weight. For
most, this will be a good thing. For some, it will bring along with it

cardiovascular issues when they go from sitting behind a desk all day to having to cut firewood and haul water.

With that in mind, one of the best things we can do for ourselves is get in shape. Cut those extra pounds now and get some exercise into your life.

Start with a daily walk and gradually increase the distance. When you're able to walk five miles without keeling over, add your pack to the walk. That extra weight will make a difference and probably cut back on your distance. But the entire reason you have the pack is to potentially carry it to get home. So, doesn't it only make sense to actually be able to carry it?

Preventative Maintenance

Now is the time, when everything is working as it should, to get those little annoying medical issues addressed. Have a cavity? Get to the dentist post haste. A simple filling today can prevent an abscess that leads to sepsis and a horrible death in a grid-down world. Get your teeth cleaned regularly and remember, finding a dentist post-collapse will be like finding a unicorn.

It's not just our teeth we need to think about though. Something as simple as plantar fasciitis could prevent you from making even a short hike home. Getting an annual physical and taking care of any issues that arise then will pay dividends later. Yes, it can be inconvenient. Yes, it is can also be expensive. But, what's your life worth? What's your vision or your ability to chew food worth? I'd say priceless. And, if you're the person others are going to be depending on when the balloon goes up, you owe it not only to yourself, but to them as well. What good will you be if you're laid up with a hernia that you've known about for three years but didn't bother to address? Go to the doc. Get your health in order. All the preps in the world will not solve these small issues that a little time and money can today.

Also consider you vices/addictions. When goods are no longer accessible/available, a heavy drinker may experience delirium tremors

(DTs), which can be fatal. When cigarettes are no longer available, coffee, tea (pray the Gods no!), chocolate (Alan says this is simply unacceptable!)—choose your drug, you are not going to feel or act like the person you are now. Someone suffering from DTs or acute withdrawal is not an asset to your group.

You could find yourself being no longer welcome if you've become a raving lunatic due to withdrawal. Start now to moderate and stop those habits that became addictions. Now, while you can taper off of them with the use of readily available over-the-counter remedies to aid in your path to having a healthier lifestyle; do it now! You will have enough stress on your plate in a crisis; don't let withdrawal make it worse.

The IFAK

The IFAK, or Individual First-Aid Kit, is an essential piece of gear for the modern individual interested in preparedness. There are endless articles and YouTube videos on what should be in one and what they are for. Preppers, in general, have the idea of this little pouch all wrong. In all probability, it is not going to save your life. However, it can prolong it, and that is its real purpose.

Now, before the gnashing of teeth begins, let's look at the typical IFAK. The IFAK generally consists of a trauma dressing, with the Israeli pressure dressing being the most common. They generally, and should always, have a tourniquet (TQ) as well. A nasopharyngeal airway (NPA) and a couple of chest seals usually round it out, along with a pair of nitrile gloves on top and possibly a clotting agent of some sort. What are these items designed to do?

The pressure dressing is used to cover a trauma wound, like a gun shot. Properly employed, they apply pressure directly to the wound, the first thing we do to stop bleeding, as well as covering with a sterile dressing. If this doesn't stop the bleeding, we move to the TQ. The tourniquet is used when a pressure dressing can't get the job done.

If the pressure dressing is insufficient to staunch the bleeding, then in all probability a vein or artery has been damaged. Arterial bleeding is pretty obvious most of the time. The human heart is a very strong muscle and when an artery is opened, it can spurt blood a considerable distance. Once the TQ has been applied, the clock is running. Modern studies have confirmed that a TQ can remain in place much longer than previously thought. However, this is predicated on the idea that a higher level of care is available. In a grid-down world, there is no nine-line coming, no EMS, no 911; no one is coming to save you.

The chest seals in our IFAK are to treat a penetrating wound to the lung. When a lung is pierced, air escapes it and enters the chest cavity. This pressure slowly constricts how far the lung can expand until there is so much air in the chest that the lung is fully compromised and unable to inflate at all. Applying a chest seal stops air from entering through the entry wound. But to get the air out of the chest cavity, we need a decompression needle, which should also be part of your IFAK. This is inserted between the ribs on the same side of the victim's chest as the puncture wound to allow that air to escape the chest cavity and permit the lung to fully inflate. This isn't something you're going to learn on the fly. You *must* have proper training to attempt such treatment and even then, only as a last resort against certain death.

If our victim's airway is compromised, that's where the NPA comes in. The NPA comes with a small packet of water-based lubricant. Squirt this into your gloved hand and coat the outside of the tube with it. If you don't have the lube, use the victim's blood; it doesn't matter, it's their blood. Or worst case, spit into your hand. The next part is where most people mess up. It is common to see people stick the tube straight into the nostril in an attempt to insert it, this would be very incorrect. Instead of going straight in, we need to aim down, with the tube against the top of the nostril, towards the ear or the back of the throat, as that is where it will end up. Do not push too hard or you can rupture the mucus membrane and cause severe bleeding. If one nostril doesn't work easily, try the other.

Tilt the victim's head back and gently insert the tube using a gentle twisting motion to make the turn in the nasal cavity. If the victim begins breathing on their own, awesome. If not, they will need to be ventilated. For this, you will need a Bag Valve Mask (BVM), also known as an Ambu Bag, to do the job. If you don't have one, it's good ole rescue breathing. This is not a big deal if someone falls over in the garden but is something else entirely if it's in the middle of a firefight.

Now, why did I say these items weren't meant to save your life but to extend it? Because if you have to use any of this on yourself or a teammate, they almost certainly will die. If you're in a fight and an artery takes a hit and you have to use a TQ, the best you can hope for is for that injured person to be able to stay in the fight long enough to make a difference. Maybe they cover the retreat of the rest of the group. Maybe a hard goodbye is said, and the group recovers most of the wounded members' gear and has to move out.

At this point, I know some of you are saying, *there's no way I'd leave my buddies behind!* An admirable quality for sure. I'd like my friends to think that. I'd also really like for my friends not to get killed trying to save my ass then and there only to die a miserable, painful death later. Think about it; with the sort of wounds we're talking about, do you have the ability to treat them? Do you have a surgical suite with all the instruments? An autoclave on standby to keep those instruments sterile? Do you have an x-ray machine or CT scanner to get a look at that internal damage? No? Then it's 1800s level medicine for you, "ditch medicine."

Alan and I have talked at length about this subject. He's a big guy, sixsix and nearly 250 pounds. I'm just over six feet and about the same. Could I drag him out of a fight? Could he drag me out? Maybe. But I don't want to find out and damn sure don't want him dying in the attempt. I'd prefer he took my rifle and ammo and got away while I used my pistol to try and keep the other guy's head down. Hard choice? Absolutely. But when you step back and look at it realistically, it's the hard truth. Without modern medicine, people are going to die from very preventable issues.

And since I know the comparisons to the Civil War will come up, let's address them now. Yes, people survived horrific wounds during the Civil War. The projectiles were huge, normally fifty caliber or larger. Artillery caused the most wounds. While those black powder shells were relatively weak compared to today's ordinance, they got the job done.

Today's weaponry is far more lethal than those cap and ball rifles of the past. High velocity rifles cause massive trauma. Explosives of today, even improvised, are more effective than the old black powder charges used in that period. The wounds will be far more severe than what we saw then. Sure, some people will survive wounds that should be a death sentence. The recovery will be long, painful and fraught with danger for both the victim and the caregivers.

There will be severe mental fatigue on caregivers who will probably be family members or very close friends. They will feel helpless as they sit and watch a loved one suffer in agonizing pain and have nothing on hand to relieve it. Infections will take most of them. The victims will be delirious as their minds are scorched by raging fever as their bodies try to fight off the infection.

It will not be pretty. As a matter of fact, it will be horrific. You will need an immense amount of bandaging material and ways to sterilize instruments and other items that will come in contact with wounds. Not to mention, the personnel requirements of providing that care. What if the wounded individual is the most skilled and useful person in the group? What will you do if that one person you rely on more than others gets wounded? Who can step in and take their place? Who else will have their level of knowledge? What will happen to the rest of the group?

Be prepared to lose group members. If you're going into this thinking you will never suffer a casualty, you need a reality check. Remember, the other side gets a vote as well. And their plans are entirely different than yours. Plan accordingly.

Got Your shots?

While there is much discussion around vaccinations, there are some shots we should have. Tetanus is one of those shots we should all have. Sure, it'll wear off, but let's stack the deck in our favor. The biggest misconception about tetanus is that you get it when you cut yourself on a piece of rusty metal. And while this is certainly one vector for the disease, it's not the only or even most common. The bacteria that causes tetanus, Clostridium tetani is most often found in soil, dust and animal feces. Cutting yourself on a piece of metal is certainly one way, but the most common way is through a puncture wound such as stepping on a nail barefoot.

Tetanus presents itself in a number of ways. Stiffness of the neck, jaw and other muscles. It is often accompanied by a sneering or grinning expression. Because of the issues in the jaw, the victim develops difficulty swallowing as a result of uncontrolled spasms, which can occur in any muscle group. Sweating and fever also come with the fun. The spasms can affect the chest and diaphragm, which potentially could lead to death. The shot is good for five years, make sure you stay up to date.

Back to the Not so Good Ole Days

In a grid-down scenario, we will essentially be operating under 1800s levels of medicine. The hospitals will be gone, so will the pharmacies, Doc in a Box and every other convenience of today. Yes, people in the 1800s survived terrible wounds; they were the exception and not the rule. The strong survive and the weak will die. During the Civil War, limbs were amputated in volume. If a femoral artery was hit, the standard treatment was amputation. Could you amputate a leg or arm from a loved one without the benefit of anesthesia, sterile instruments or knowledge of anatomy? Probably not. Those doctors of the 1800s did at least have this knowledge, even if they didn't understand things like blood-borne pathogens and disease vectors. They still knew how to cut that leg off, prevent blood loss that would result in shock and death, and close the wound properly.

The number one thing the survivor can do to maintain quality health is to properly address sanitation needs. Poor sanitary habits are the number one disease vector in densely populated areas, disaster areas and conflict zones. When the modern sanitary systems fail, people get sick. While easily prevented, most people today have no idea what to do with their waste if the toilet doesn't flush. Get organized now to handle your sanitation.

Even if you do have your sanitation situation squared away, your neighbors may not. Keep that in mind. Flies landing on the neighbors' improperly disposed-of feces then flying over your privacy fence and landing on your dinner plate will have the same result. Do everything you can to keep clean. Soap should be a high priority. Keeping your body, cooking and eating utensils, clothing and bedding clean will go a long way toward keeping you healthy.

Pills, Powders, and Potions

We need to be prepared to deal with whatever comes our way. Having a small pharmacy at home will put us ahead of the game. Items like Tylenol are taken for granted today. They can be had at any corner store and nearly everyone has a bottle rolling around in their car or purse. Having stocks of over-the-counter medications is necessary. Everything from pain relievers to anti-diarrheal medications will be very important in a crisis.

Bandaging Material

While a majority of folks in prepping focus on the potential medical emergencies arising from combat related injuries, they will be infrequent in occurrence, but severe in result. What we are more likely to face will be daily injuries from conducting the chores required to live in this new world. Physical labor will be the biggest source of injury.

One of the most common injuries will be burns. Treatment of burns requires a lot of dressing material. Other wounds such as cuts, severe lacerations from things like knives, axes and chainsaws will also occur. These kinds of wounds also require a lot of bandaging material to treat.

You will need enormous amounts of gauze, both rolled and pads, non-adherent dressings, abdominal pads (ABD) pads for heavy bleeding and tape. Like water and firewood, you can never have too much of these items.

Adding in bottles of betadine as well as some sterile saline solution to your preps will allow you to keep wounds irrigated and clean. Have a couple of large irrigation syringes, the type without needles, to be able to properly wash out a deep wound. In a pinch, fill a plastic bag with the sterile solution and snip off a corner and squeeze the bag to produce the pressure needed to wash out the wound.

Wound treatment and being able to keep it clean and dry will be the most important part of the process. Access to medical services may be limited or nonexistent; be prepared to treat even severe wounds yourself.

Sutures

This is another topic that I believe is overrated. Everyone wants to learn to suture and to have kits on hand. While we all should have some of this material available, we should not be under the impression we're going to be sewing up every wound we find. Closing a wound is tricky business. It's often an invitation to infection. What we should learn about is what's called secondary intention. In this method, we leave the wound open; it must be debrided of foreign bodies such as grass or dirt, and dead or disconnected tissue needs to be excised. Once cleaned, the wound should be packed with sterile gauze soaked in saline and covered with sterile bandages. The wound will granulate, adding additional protection. It is irrigated, cleaned and redressed daily. The wound will heal from the inside out. While this will leave a substantial scar, it helps reduce the chance of infection to a large degree.

Sutures should be saved for things like tying off an artery should you be forced to amputate a limb. Did that scare you? It should. Because it could happen. Think about the possibility of having to do that, what it would look like, what it would sound like as your friend, spouse or child lay there screaming as you worked to remove a limb without benefit of anesthesia or subsequent pain relief. That's how desperate we should be before we take up stitching on people.

I know a lot of you are saying, *but I took a suture class! I learned to sew up a pig's foot!* Great! How long ago was that? When was the last time you practiced that skillset? Was there subcutaneous damage as well that required the use of absorbable sutures as well as non-absorbable sutures to close the skin? You did learn the difference, didn't you? And you have the proper materials on hand, including sterile drapes to keep the suture sterile as you sew to prevent dragging bacteria into the wound. In that class, your pig was dead when you learned to sew up its foot and in all likelihood you weren't sterile and didn't learn anything about maintaining a sterile field. Suturing, like any skill, is perishable in that the longer you go between utilizing that skillset, the worse you'll perform. Skills must be maintained, just like working out to maintain physical condition. We must exercise our skills, or they will atrophy over time.

Clean Water and Soap

These items have already been discussed at length, but we'll emphasize them one more time. You simply cannot have enough soap and access to clean water. Any water used to treat wounds should be boiled first to sterilize it. If you've run out of bandaging material, you can boil bed sheets, old t-shirts or whatever you have to make sterile bandaging. You can also boil and reuse bandaging if necessary. This has been a common practice throughout history during wars.

Keeping wounds clean will be critical. Caregivers being meticulous with handwashing both before and after wound care and dressing changes is paramount. We don't want to introduce bacteria into the wound, and we don't want to spread anything that may already be there. So, wash your hands before and after interacting with the wounded. Also, stock nitrile exam gloves!

Illness

People get sick every day; it happens all the time. They will get sick in a crisis as well. While a crisis may reduce the number of people we come into contact with on a daily basis, thereby reducing the chance of *catching* whatever they have, it also forces us to live in substandard conditions. Sanitation will naturally not be what we're used to, and we'll all have to exercise extreme caution to avoid getting sick.

Diarrhea is the number one cause of death around the underdeveloped world. Improper sanitation and a lack of cleaning supplies is a breeding ground for disease. Children in particular are very susceptible to this. Once it starts, if it isn't controlled, they will die of dehydration.

The only method that will be available for most will be oral rehydration. The World Health Organization has a revised recipe for the solution that lowered the amount of sodium and other ingredients to allow for faster absorption of the water into the body. The ingredients are simple, cheap and readily available. They consist of clean water, salt, sugar, salt substitute and trisodium citrate dihydrate. This last one may sound exotic, but it's simply a salt of citric acid. This is easily available on Amazon today.

Oral Rehydration Recipe

- ½ teaspoon salt
- 2 tablespoons plus ¾ teaspoon sugar
- ½ teaspoon Morton's salt substitute
- 1¼ teaspoons trisodium citrate dihydrate

This solution should be constantly sipped during waking hours. The goal is to produce at least a liter of urine from the afflicted over a twenty-four-hour period. This solution does not store well and should be discarded after twenty-four hours and a new batch made.

There are also commercially available solutions such as CeraLyte 70, Trioral rehydration salts and even Gatorade can be used by adding an additional ½ teaspoon of salt to a quart of the drink; shake well and it's ready to use. (Source: The Oley Foundation, https://cdn.ymaws.com/oley.org/ resource/resmgr/ors_recipes/ORS_recipes_handout.pdf)

Childbirth

It is so common after a natural disaster for there to be a spike in births in the affected area that it's now used as a joke. Living in Florida and having weathered several hurricanes, we've all heard the jokes about *hurricane babies*, and science backs it up. Studies have been done that show a spike in childbirth nine months after a disaster. The power is out, the roads are blocked and entertainment opportunities are limited. So, people will do what people do.

Stay ahead of this by storing prophylactics. Yes, the good ole rubber will be the number one method to prevent unwanted pregnancy. I would recommend ladies that are still fertile learn their cycle and learn the rhythm method. This is one of the oldest methods of birth control. However, it is very important to remember than sperm can live in the female body for up to five days. So, learning your cycle will help with prevention. There are several apps today available for women to track their cycle. I would also recommend keeping a written calendar as a backup.

Mechanical Injury

With most people today working in professions that do not require a lot of physical labor, they are not physically prepared for a sudden shift into a more physical lifestyle. Weak joints and muscles will result in numerous mechanical injuries. Back injuries will be common due to people's physical condition and trying to do too much. Twisted ankles, sprained wrists and even broken bones will be common. And while most of these are rather benign, a broken bone can be a severe issue.

Setting a bone is a painful process. Traction must be applied to the affected bone to reset it. Then casting material must be applied. You can get this material online from a number of sources. However, learning to set a bone is going to take training. I would highly recommend looking into such training. Also, keeping plenty of Ace Bandages and wrapping tape is highly recommended.

Burns

Burns will be one of the most common injuries we see in post-disaster and grid-down scenarios. People not used to interacting with fire on a daily basis will get burned. Children in particular will suffer burns as they are young and, in many cases, totally unaware of the dangers of fire. Be very cautious of using candles and lanterns in the kids' rooms. Many children are burned when an ignition source falls onto their bedding. This also leads to the danger fire presents to our homes.

Modern homes are not designed to be heated by fire. There's an active campaign in many states to actually outlaw fireplaces all together. Improvised methods of using fire to heat a home will surely lead to either a fire or smoke inhalation or even carbon monoxide poisoning. If you're going to try and improvise a stove in your home, take a lot of time to think it out. Ensure your home is properly vented to allow fresh air in and that the exhaust isn't leaking into your home. Carbon monoxide poisoning is deadly and, in most cases, unknown until it's too late. It is a completely odorless and tasteless gas.

Burns are categorized by the degree of their severity. First degree burns are considered the least severe because they only affect the outer layer of skin. This comes from touching a hot pan or even sunburn. Second degree burns affect deeper layers of skin and cause blisters and white, wet and shiny skin. These are far more painful. Third degree burns affect all layers of the skin and into the muscle tissue below and fourth degree burns will include joints and bones. These last two are considered severe medical emergencies and require aggressive treatment.

The basic treatment for burns is to cool the area immediately with cool, not cold, water. Place the burn under running water or use cold compresses. You can apply an antibiotic ointment to firstand second-degree burns; however, do not pop any blisters that may occur. While the blisters may look awful, they are still intact skin. Popping them will create another open wound where infection can take hold.

Aloe vera is a great resource for burns. It is anti-inflammatory, promotes circulation and inhibits bacterial growth. Simply cut open a leaf and squeeze the gel out directly onto the wound and cover it with a non-adherent dressing. Avoid sun exposure for all degrees of burns and remember, never pop the blisters.

For thirdand fourth-degree burns, the treatment is far more involved. These burns will be very difficult to treat yourself. They require debridement (removal of dead skin and tissue), intravenous fluids and antibiotics and daily dressing changes. When the dressing is removed, additional debridement is conducted. The bandaging commonly sticks to the weeping wounds and this process is extremely painful. Should a victim suffer such a burn, it will be a very long process to get them healed, if it's at all possible. You will not be able to conduct skin grafts. The skin is the first line of defense for our immune system. When it's been compromised to such an extreme degree, infection is almost a certainty. Antibiotics will certainly be required, and oral treatment may not be sufficient. Treat all burns with the utmost care and paramount urgency.

Medical issues will certainly arise. We must prepare ourselves to deal with them. If you know a doctor or have one in the family, ask them to provide you with a list of the sort of items you should store as well as requesting prescriptions for antibiotics and even pain relievers. I cannot stress enough how much bandaging material you should store. Every time you go to the store, you should be adding to these stocks. Even the Dollar Store sells bandaging material and it's fairly cheap there. No matter where you choose to purchase these materials, just buy them!

And, as previously mentioned, don't forget things like over-the-counter meds, antibiotic ointments, cough suppressants, Benadryl, Imodium and other medicines that should be stored away. There will be no ER to rush to in the middle of the night. There will be no 911; no one is coming to save you. *You are your own first responder!*

15 - Bartering & Bickering

*The propensity to truck, barter and exchange one
thing for another… is common to all men, and
to be found in no other race of animals.*
—Adam Smith, *Wealth of Nations*

B ARTERING GOES BACK TO THE dawn of man. It's the oldest method of acquiring what one needs when they either cannot be produced or simply lack the time, skill or resources to do so. This is an often discussed and generally misunderstood practice. Many people in the prepper world think of bartering as a near utopian idea. Where markets will be set up and people will interact freely in the open to trade their wares or surplus for what they want and need. The reality looks a little different.

In a collapsed or collapsing society, bartering, which can also mean black market, will become the method of exchange. The rules will always be in flux, as will prices and the items available. The only constant in bartering is there isn't one. It is often fraught with danger and not something to be entered into hastily. A barter must be entered into with the same amount of planning as any other operation the survivor must conduct. By establishing some hard and fast rules, you can stack the odds in your favor. Never trade from your home location, ever. The only exception to this would be with family or tribe members that are fully trusted, to the point they have full access to your location. Anyone outside of that circle must be treated with suspicion and distrust; it's the nature of the game. Likewise, never trade on the other's home turf either. You are giving them all of the advantages and you will be at a distinct disadvantage. Decide on a neutral location ahead of time if possible. Agree on the price of the trade ahead of time as well if at all possible. You should also agree on the number of people that will be attending the barter; you will always want security, as will the other side.

When you approach a trade, try and look like everyone else. Depending on the situation, it may be a mistake to roll up in full kit with shiny weapons, nice boots and looking fit as a fiddle. While a show of force has its place, it will potentially make you a target. Never give anyone a reason to risk a fight with you. At the same time, don't walk in looking meek and vulnerable for a couple of reasons. One, if you look desperate, prices will go up. Also, if you look weak, the other side may just decide to rip you off and take your stuff and be on their way. Stay away from extremes; we're trying to strike a balance here.

On the thought of desperation, never trade from that position. If at all possible, treat the trade as though it's your second or third choice. Act as if it's not what you really want, but you'll take it. Do not carry more than the agreed-on price with you and if possible, spread that around. This is one way to cover your assets. Do not keep all your money, gold or whatever you're trading in one pocket. Spread it out in multiple pockets, in your shoe, belt, hat or among your companions.

Avoid trading with the same person too often, until trust is established. Word will get around that you have a lot of stuff, and that makes you a target. Just like trading the same item to multiple people, word will spread that you've got lots of coffee for instance; again, this could make you a target. Also, do not trade in the same place too often; this establishes a pattern that can be exploited.

A good way to mitigate this is to act as a middleman, as the guy that knows a guy. First, it takes the attention away from you. Second, there will always be a finder's fee involved with such transactions. You knowing that Jim down the street really needs flints for a Zippo lighter and that Steve across town has them, puts you in a position to profit. Expect a fee if you're dealing with a middleman. Acting as though there is one involved offers you a level of cover.

Security when trading is paramount. Alternate your routes in and out. Know who has what, who is a good guy and who rips people off; conduct your HUMINT (human intelligence) and build a picture. Make sure you're not being followed home from a trade as this will surely end up with your home being besieged for its contents. When people have nothing, anything can make you a target; use your head.

One last note on bartering. If you have never heard of Selco, look him up. He lived through the Bosnian conflict in a city surrounded and cut off for a year. For me, one of the biggest takeaways from his words was this, never give charity. I know that's going to be a hard pill to swallow for a lot of people. But in his words, it lets everyone know you had so much you could afford to give it away. If your morals simply demand you give charity, fall back to the middleman. Tell people, *I can't give you anything. But, if you go to the church on Main Street on Wednesday's at 2:00, they will.* You could be the one providing that to the church, but no one will know.

Another very important, probably the most crucial part of bartering, is the actual deal itself. Haggling over a deal in many societies is considered mandatory. Traders around the world can be insulted if you simply accept the first offer. They fully expect you to counter offer; it's about making the deal as much as anything. However, in a grid-down situation, this could cause real trouble.

Do your best to never insult the other party. Being known as the guy that rips people off or simply takes advantage of their need or desperation can become a severe liability. Sometimes it may be worth the extra cost on a deal to establish rapport with another group. Think social engineering; the trade may not even be about the items at hand. It could very well be used as cover for action to get you into a place and having a legitimate reason for being there. Remember, this works both ways. However, here again lies a risk of becoming known as a sucker that can be taken advantage of.

Approach your trading partner with respect. Do not insult them when the haggling starts; it's all part of the deal. Be polite but firm, and above all else, be ready to walk away. In many cases, simply saying, *that's just more than I can do right now, thanks*, and turning your back to leave can throw the trade into your favor. It's then you could discover which of you is the desperate one.

Bartering will become the primary method of trade. Be ready, do your homework and have a plan.

Cash, The Ultimate Survival Tool

It's a funny thing how money makes a lot of problems go away. Money talks; excrement from the bull walks. When the ATM is down, cash remains a viable option. Keeping cash on your person at all times is a solid survival strategy. When I travel abroad, I make it a practice to keep cash money in at least three places on my body. Under the insoles of your boots is a good place to keep $500 or so, just laminate it first. A money belt is also an excellent way to keep some emergency funds on hand. I prefer the one made by Wazoo Survival Gear. A few small tenth-ounce gold coins can come in handy during some circumstances.

In the survivalist/prepper community, there is much discussion around the topic of precious metals. I have nothing against precious metals (PMs), after all, they are among the few real forms of money on the planet. The historic tale of paper money is one of woe. Metals on the other hand, have always been valued. They have an intrinsic value, unlike our dollar, which is a faith-based system. Precious metals can provide protection against inflation. They are a great way to protect your wealth. But, investing in metals should be the last thing on your to-do list. There is no wisdom in sitting on a stash of gold and silver if you haven't secured your food and water.

In numerous societies around the world that have suffered calamity in modern times, cash generally retains its value for a short period. If the crisis is financial in nature and the local currency is in freefall, this could change more rapidly than you may think. Foreign currencies sometimes fill this void, but usually only for a short time. Barter usually ends up becoming the real currency. It is very hard to make change out of a one-ounce gold coin for a dozen eggs. Save your precious metals for real emergencies, such as procuring lifesaving medicines or even buying safe passage out of a hostile area.

When society is in the throes of collapse, precious metals will generally have limited value. They are bulky, heavy and difficult to conduct transactions with. The real value of precious metals is as a storage of wealth. If the dollar were to die today, you would get more new dollars with PMs than with the old dollars. This is not to say they have no place as a post-collapse currency. They would be invaluable for acquiring much needed medicines or to buy passage out of or into an area that's cut off. The last use, as unlikely as it may sound, is to pay a ransom. I personally know a young lady, now living in the US that was kidnapped twice in Venezuela. A ransom was paid the first time and a rescue operation freed her from the second. Upon being freed, she was immediately flown out of the country. It can and will happen.

When a society collapses, and law goes out the window, the world will change in ways that may be hard for you to imagine now. Kidnapping is a very common occurrence under such conditions. The reasons vary; it could be motivated strictly by money, or for human trafficking. In Syria, when ISIS was seizing vast swaths of territory, it wasn't uncommon for Christian or Yazidi families to buy their way out of the territory. Staying meant certain death for the men and a life of slavery for the women with all the terrible connotations that come with that. A little gold or silver could mean the difference between life and death and that is why money truly is the ultimate survival tool.

16 - Consumables

When that terrible day comes, what you have is all you will have.
Plan accordingly.
—Angery American

W E LIVE IN A WONDERFUL society where anything the
heart desires is nothing more than a click away. Think
about that; you can have nearly anything you want delivered to your doorstep with no more effort than the manipulation of
your index finger! No longer must you toil away in labor to create what
you need. In the past, to feed your family, you had to clear the land
of trees and stack them for later use. Dig out the stones and pile them
for fences. Then plow that ground, plant the seed and tend your crops.
When harvest time came around, you had to go out and pick that crop,
process it and prepare it for storage. This took years. The planting and
harvesting processes alone took many months. Now, you can sit on
your sofa and Shipt will deliver it to your door.

This all works because of the mind-bogglingly complex society to
which we belong. Complexity creates fragility. The more complex any
system, the more opportunities for failure there are. The sheer weight
and complexity of the modern systems we use to obtain the vast variety of items we humans need to sustain ourselves is simply unsustainable. Therefore, we must plan for the eventual failure of these systems.

Think of it like your car. You know the gas tank only holds so much, and before it runs out, you better have a plan.

There is simply no way we can store all the things we will need throughout our lives. But it is incumbent upon us to at least try to mitigate the discomfort and potential life-threatening situations that could easily arise from not being prepared to the best of our abilities and budgets. And it doesn't have to be expensive, there are cheap ways of stocking our warehouses.

I will not attempt to cover everything that we should be considering. That work alone would look like the entire collection of the Encyclopedia Britannica. The goal here is to cause you to think about things you would normally dismiss as mere junk.

Some of the categories we need to consider are hardware, plumbing supplies, lumber, rolls of plastic and hand tools. I do not mean battery-powered cordless drills. A brace and bit will run as long as you have the strength to turn it. Crosscut saws will never run out of fuel. You may be thinking you have no intention of taking on construction projects. And that's not why we're talking about storing these things.

Right now, if a storm comes through and blows a couple shingles off of the roof, it's no big deal to run to the local hardware store and get some more. Or if the trash pandas, *see also raccoons,* find their way into the chicken coop, hitting up the local feed store for more wire is easy enough. But what happens when we no longer have those resources? Those missing shingles now become a leaking roof and the trash pandas get fed while you and your family potentially go hungry.

In a world where you will heat your home, cook your food, heat water for sanitation and other numerous tasks that fire will accomplish for us, a broken axe handle could be a real crisis. Do you have a spare? This also applies to shovels, hoes to work the garden and spare tubes for the wheelbarrow tire. We have to think broadly and take these things into consideration. Or, you could just buy an airless tire and circumvent the whole problem.

I think most people overlook clothing and footwear. How many pairs of boots do you have? Does everyone in your family have rugged footwear? When your world is reduced to how far you can walk in a day, you must have adequate footwear to make that happen. Do you have replacements? In our current world, clothing and shoes are more about fashion than function. In an alternate world where your days are filled with hard work, do you have the clothing and footwear that will stand up to the abuse? People spend hundreds on jeans that someone in Asia "distressed" to make them look cool. You won't have to worry about that in the world I'm talking about. You'll instead be looking for ways to repair those holes to keep that pair of jeans in service a little longer.

Keep this in mind, the number one thing requested in homeless shelters around the country is socks. Socks and underwear are something we take for granted, despite the fact Alan hasn't owned a pair of underwear in twenty plus years! Most people go to one of the big retailers and buy these in fat packs for next to nothing. They are cheaply made and do not last long. I would highly recommend rotating these cheap versions out for higher quality. Companies like Darn Tough make socks built for work that will stand up to the abuse. But even these will wear out, so plan ahead and start stocking up on them.

And this brings us to our children. If you have small kids at home or even older ones who may be in the midst of their growing spurt, do you have the shoes and clothes to see them through? If suddenly today, right now, you no longer had access to stores to replace their clothes as they rapidly outgrow them, could you keep them clothed? Could you keep shoes on their feet? It was common in earlier decades in this nation that you got one new pair of shoes a year and that was it. You had one pair that you wore to school, to church, to play and work in. Think ahead and get a few sizes up and put them away.

All this sounds like a lot, and it is. You're probably going through a mental list in your head right now and thinking, *there is no way I can do all this*. And you're right; you'll never have it all. There is no way to obtain and store everything you could ever possibly need. But any steps you take will make a difference. And this doesn't have to break the bank either. Hit up yard sales, thrift stores and the like. Flea markets are a good place to find decent used items as well.

I like to hit yard sales and look for those buckets of miscellaneous parts when someone cleans out their garage or workshop. They dump all this loose stuff into a bucket and sell the whole thing. It could have nails, screws, hardware parts and even PVC fittings. These can generally be had for next to nothing and really add to the inventory of on-hand supplies for emergency repairs. The same yard sale could yield junior a couple pairs of shoes two sizes up and maybe even a pair of jeans that he'll grow into in a couple of years.

We do not throw out old clothes in my house. We put them in the big Zip-Lok bags that can be compressed using a vacuum and put into storage. Those old jeans may not be in style now, but in a world where there are no more malls, you'll be glad you have them and happily wear them. These are just some of the things that we need to think about; and you really need to assess your personal situation. Just approach it from the viewpoint of, *how would I solve these problems if I couldn't just run out and buy what I need?* That is coming. It may be ten years from now or next month; we just don't know. But every step you take today puts you that much further ahead.

17 - The Juice

When there is no power, a little goes a long way.
—Angery American

LIFE IS ENERGY. WE, AS humans consume and produce energy. Our bodies generate heat; this is energy. Our muscles require calories, energy, to create physical energy to manipulate the world around us.

The cars we drive burn fuel, liquid energy, to create propulsion, velocity, which is also energy. This glorious planet we live on survives on the energy created by our sun. Life is energy and like water, without energy, there is no life.

In our modern lives, a lot of the energy we use is hidden from us. Power is delivered to our homes through cables, either strung through the air or buried underground. We do not see the source of the energy, only its manifestation in the form of lights, heat, refrigeration and air conditioning. When we are tasked with the production of our own energy, things become much more difficult.

The most fundamental form of energy is heat. Burning things, be it wood, coal or oil, produces heat energy. We use this to cook our food, to render our water safe to drink and to maintain our body's core temperature. These are all things necessary for a human to stay healthy and alive. And since burning fuel is the most basic form of creating energy, we need to consider this.

For millennia, man used fire as the sole source of providing all these needs. In a collapse situation, we could well be faced with that prospect once again. Sadly, modern homes are not constructed in a manner to easily facilitate this. Few homes today have fireplaces, and fewer still have wood stoves. How will you heat your modern home when the power goes out or the gas stops flowing?

The answer is wood. Of course, you can store liquid fuels such as kerosene and liquid propane, but they will eventually run out. They are not renewable; you cannot harvest either of these from the land. Wood however has the benefit of being renewable, readily available yet laborious to obtain. It's often said that wood heats you three times. Once while you cut it, once while you split and stack it and once when you burn it.

Wood should be sourced now. Even if you're not going to cut and stack it in the garage of the house, know the closest place to find it. Have the tools with which to harvest it and a means to convey that fuel back to the homestead. Chainsaws are obviously the first choice for this task; however, they require liquid fuel and oil that will be in limited supply. Investing in a couple of quality crosscut saws and learning the skills to safely fell trees with them is critical.

In addition to the saw, there is the axe. This is the most versatile tool for the collection of wood. With it alone, you can fell a tree, clear the limbs, section it out, and split it into usable pieces. A saw makes some of this work much easier, but the axe will get the job done. Like any tool, the saw and axe will need maintenance. A good file and stone will keep them working longer than you will be able to wield them. You will definitely wear out before they do, trust me on this one.

This is not to say there is no place for liquid fuels. The reason we no longer burn wood for everything today is that these liquid fuels are more efficient and burn cleaner. Putting up a stock of gasoline, diesel and propane is a wise move. In a collapse situation, they are also powerful barter material. With gas and some oil, you can keep your chainsaw running for quite some time. Diesel will keep the tractor going to tend the fields. Propane will provide heat and a way to cook indoors without exhaust being an issue.

When dealing with these fuels, prepare them for storage and develop a rotation schedule. Gasoline that has been properly treated will store between one and three years under ideal conditions before degradation renders it useless. Airtight containers stored out of direct sunlight will lengthen their shelf life. The various fuel additives will go a long way in maintaining the viability of these precious liquids.

Solar is another option that may be expensive on the front end but can pay dividends on the back end. Once a solar system is properly set up, it will run uninterrupted for many years with minimal maintenance. However, they are not the silver bullet of energy. These are complex systems that the average person will not be able to repair if there is a major failure.

Should you decide to invest in such a system, I highly recommend you do it yourself. If you hire a contractor, spend time with them during the installation to learn as much as you can about it. There are a number of components to these systems that are complex. Charge controllers, inverters and batteries are all failure points. It's a good idea to have spares for all of these on the shelf. Batteries can be purchased dry, with the electrolyte bottled and ready to be added.

Once your system is up and running, it will silently provide power for you. This is a low signature option as compared to a generator. They can be limited by cloud cover, snow or storms that can degrade their production for days at a time. Keep this in mind and do not become too reliant on them.

I like to say that when there is no power, a little power is a lot. Even a couple of car batteries connected in parallel to one another with a small charge controller and a hundred-watt solar panel will provide substantial power. Adding an inverter will broaden the usability by converting that stored DC power into AC. Bear in mind, that when using an inverter there is a sizeable loss of power during the conversion process so, the more you can do with DC, the better.

The best use for small systems like this is to keep batteries charged.

Having a supply of rechargeable batteries for things like flashlights, radios, optics and even cordless tools can make life a lot easier. There are even DC appliances available that have made leaps and bounds in the last few years in efficiency and performance.

Start thinking now about your real power needs. If you approach it from the position that you want to maintain your life exactly as it is now, you will more than likely end up sadly disappointed. We are energy-spoiled today. Think about what you really need to do with power and plan accordingly.

18 - Down Time

D URING ANY CRISIS, WE ARE stressed out. And when we get stressed out, our kids will get stressed out, which will only serve to stress us further. With this thought in mind, it's important to plan ahead and make sure we have some healthy distractions available for everyone involved. There will be times when all the work is done and we're alone with our thoughts and fears.

In our modern world, we live in a near constant state of distraction. There's no end of electronic devices to distract us when we have that spare moment. Simply reach into your pocket and there it is. The answer to any question you have is within your grasp! Think about that. Not to mention, you can always immediately pull up a video to watch for entertainment and educational purposes.

During a crisis, however, this luxury may not be available to us. That doesn't mean that every crisis will knock us back to the 1800s; but we should be ready for that. Analog is great because it nearly always works. And by analog, I mean anything that isn't electronic. Having entertainment options that do not rely on batteries is a hole in many people's preps.

This is particularly important for the little ones. Having distractions around for smaller children can bring a lot of harmony to the homestead. Sure, they should be helping out, they should be included in the chores that are age appropriate for them. Feeding the chickens and collecting the eggs is something any seven-year-old can do. Here in the west, we underestimate our kids. They are far more capable than we give them credit for. It's just become popular in recent decades to treat them as completely incapable individuals that need to be sheltered and protected. We could write an entire book on that subject.

As stated earlier, not every crisis will mean the complete loss of electricity. Having a stock of DVDs around is one great way to ensure we have a positive distraction for those long quiet nights. I would go more with comedies and feel-good movies and possibly action flicks that do not speak to the situation at hand. Even if the power is out, a portable DVD/Blue Ray player or laptop can fill the bill nicely. A small solar set up can run and charge these easily enough.

Some other options would be board games, of all varieties. As well as decks of cards and card games such as Uno. These need nothing more than a flat spot and a little light to play. We've all played that game of Monopoly that went on for two or more days. Something like that can keep morale up as it can be a long-term distraction for several days. Just like a chess board set up on a table with a running game that the participants can stop and ponder a move and make it before carrying on with their daily routine. Then the other player can do likewise. Games played in this manner take longer to play and can increase the competitiveness and enjoyment as opposed to just sitting in front of the board for long stretches.

For kids, keeping a few new, unopened and age appropriate toys in your stores can be a sanity saver. Every kid loves getting a new toy and being able to hand them something brand new in the midst of a crisis can be a great way to distract them for a while. Just keep them rotated out for birthdays, Christmas or even as a reward during normal times. This will ensure they are appropriate for their age when they get them and even save you from having to run to the store when they come home from school and tell you they've been invited to a birthday party that starts in two hours!

If you have a hobby that lends itself well to storing components, then do so. Knitting, wood carving, pottery and many other pastimes can fill those down hours and allow a sense of normalcy. Not to mention pay dividends by producing something useful in the current situation. Lay in a stock of paper, sketchbooks, pens, markers and crayons. These can be used by anyone. Paints and canvases are another great idea. Just rotate them into your normal daily use now and they won't be degraded when you want to paint something during a crisis.

The last thing I'll mention is having a good library. Include fiction books. Not only for entertainment but for valuable how-to knowledge. The internet may be gone and the only resource you'll have available will be books. I personally, and I know Alan does as well, have a rather diversified collection of books on a vast array of topics. These can also become a community reference, turning them into a barterable item. I wouldn't let any of them get away from me but would allow people (that are trusted) to look them over to answer questions. If your friends and neighbors are readers as well, you can trade books back and forth, giving you something other than the daily needs to talk about, adding yet another distraction for you and those around you.

These are just a few ideas of things to consider. The point here is to think about what you and the family will be doing during those long dark nights. Being able to distract yourself for an hour or two and totally forget about what's going on at the moment provides a much-needed mental escape. You simply cannot stay switched-on all the time. You will wear yourself down. Your nerves will fray, and you'll become less effective at everything you do. So, plan ahead now to fill those hours and maintain your sanity.

19 - Hygiene

Since the Middle Ages, progress in hygiene has
been characterized by the conquest of stink.
—Martin H. Fischer

H YGIENE AND SANITATION ARE AMONG the most essential priorities for optimal human health. The longer they are absent, the more their necessity will be realized. We often take for granted the daily occurrences that enable us to remain clean and free from avoidable disease. What enables you to clean your body? Water is piped in from another location directly into your home. Soap and other products are purchased using your vehicle and fuel to travel to obtain them. Money, or some other financial medium, makes the transaction possible.

Human waste is swept away using copious amounts of water and electricity. We are blessed with some of the cleanest water in the world here in America. Outside our borders, and to a degree inside them, that isn't the case; *think Flint, Michigan.* The World Health Organization estimates that five thousand children die every day from lack of clean water and every twenty-one seconds a child dies from waterborne disease.

A UNIFEC report found that over six million people today are blind from Trachoma, a waterborne pathogen resulting from lack of clean water and poor sanitation standards. Clean water is so ubiquitous that we take it for granted. So spoiled are we that we won't even drink our tap water. In 2011, Americans spent nearly *twelve billion dollars* on bottled water that in many cases comes from the same municipal water supplies piped into their homes at pennies on the dollar. Water is life; without water, there is no life. When the grid goes down, where will your water come from?

We obviously need water to keep ourselves clean. Lots of prepper types store food and other supplies; be sure to store soaps as well. Liquid soaps such as dish detergent are quite versatile. Such soaps can be used to clean your body, clothes, car, the floor and countertops and of course, the dishes. We all remember the commercials by Dawn dish soap of the baby ducklings covered in oil being gently cleaned with their product. There's a reason it was used; stock up.

Feminine hygiene products are an essential prep item; do not overlook them. And like many items we try to store, this is another where no matter how much you stock, you will probably run out. Look to reusable products such as those made by the Lunapad company. And while some may cringe at the thought of having to wash and reuse such a product, consider the alternative of folding rags or bits of repurposed cloth. Doesn't sound so bad now, does it?

A lack of personal hygiene has crippled entire armies. Never allow such a fate to befall you and your merry band of survivors.

Human Waste

S**t happens; be ready to deal with it. If you live in one of the marvelous modern preplanned housing communities, you're probably connected to the municipal water supply and waste lines. When you flush the toilet, gravity carries your waste out to the street where it dumps into large pipes that then takes it to a lift station where a large pump, humorously called a Muffin Monster, grinds and macerates this material to make it easier to then pump to a waste treatment facility.

But what happens when the electricity required to run that monster goes out? The answer, it starts to back up. If you're one of the unfortunate souls that lives close to the lift station, that is to say you live downhill from most of your neighbors, when things start to back up, the sewage from all your neighbors will flood your house. It will come up through your bathtub and toilet and eventually inundate your entire home. Worse yet, there isn't a thing you can do to stop it.

This also, and even more profoundly, applies to high-rise buildings. These structures use gravity to get the waste to the ground where it is carried away by pipes. When the system above fails, just like the folks in the cul-de-sac, those on the lower floors will be awash in a sea of human waste.

If you live in a more rural area, you are probably on a septic system. If it is a conventional gravity system, you can control your waste with little concern. By filling the toilet tank, you can flush it away. Be aware that "flushable wipes" are not all appropriate for a septic system; they must be labeled as such. You will want to get as much time out of your septic system as possible. Remember, all the water from your toilets, bathing, and washing chores goes into the septic tank. Since you may never see another septic pump truck again, do not overtax your system. It may not be a bad idea to burn the toilet tissue as well instead of just flushing it away.

The issue with septic systems comes when you have a lift pump added to the equation. Lift pumps are used when the septic tank and drain field are higher than the floor of the house. They actually pump the waste away from the house. These are power-dependent and when the power goes out, you, like your city-dwelling neighbors, will lose the ability to remove waste from your home unless you've planned for this in your back-up power plans.

The solution to these issues will be outhouses, slit trenches and the like. You will be forced to deal with your waste yourself. It's a crappy job (no pun intended), and no one wants to do it. The alternative is not pretty, sickness, disease and death. A few things need to be considered when talking about in-ground waste disposal. You want to locate your outhouse as far from your home as you can but still be within reasonable walking distance. Nighttime trips in the dark will be inconvenient and even scary for the younger ones. Chamber pots will make a comeback.

Make sure your outhouse is located downhill from any potential water source. The pits should be dug deep, six feet is a good starting point. Keeping a bucket of wood ash nearby is another good idea. A coffee can full of wood ash kept in the outhouse and dumping a little in after each deposit will help in keeping unpleasant odors down. Keep in mind that to build an outhouse, you have to have the materials on hand to do so. Fence posts could be repurposed and wrapped in a tarp or black plastic to allow for privacy. But having an enclosed structure with a roof would be preferable, especially in winter.

The number of people using the outhouse will determine its lifespan. They will fill up and you'll be required to relocate it. Do not wait until the waste is at ground level! You'll want to be able to cover the waste with at least a couple of feet of soil. If the dirt from the original hole is no longer available, use the dirt dug out from the new location to cover the old location.

Washing Clothing and Bedding

Clothing and bedding must be kept clean to maintain a reasonable standard of health. I have washed my clothes in the creek using only sand, stones and water. Modern fragile clothing will not hold up under such harsh treatment. One expedient way to wash clothes without causing undue wear is to repurpose a five-gallon bucket. Simply cut a hole in the lid and place a toilet plunger or similar object through the hole; now you have an agitator. Place your clothing, soap and water into the bucket and actuate the plunger up and down vigorously as if churning butter. The next step requires an industrial grade mop bucket with the wringer attached. Fill the mop bucket with clean water, this will act as the rinse cycle. Place your soapy clothes into the bucket and agitate, then use the wringer to press as much water as possible out of them. This method will prove much easier than twisting your clothes by means of hands and wrists. Now take some of that 550 cord and fashion yourself a clothesline. It's too easy.

The Dead

When people die, as we all will, the call is made, and folks arrive to handle all that for you. The body is placed into a bag, sealed up, transferred to a gurney where it is further covered with a tasteful piece of cloth. You, the aggrieved family, are totally removed from the process. What happens when these systems no longer function? The answer, disease and ultimately death. Human history is littered with examples that emerge when hygiene and sanitation are absent or neglected.

The health implications of dead bodies lying around are horrific. People die every day. Burial is usually the best solution, the sooner this is done, the better. Soil conditions vary greatly depending on your location. It is essential that you have the appropriate digging implements for your area.

For example, I live in a rocky area, a shovel alone is inadequate here. A mattock or pick is essential for any serious digging project in my region.

The location of the burial site should be chosen with care. For obvious reasons, burial close to your source of drinking water is not optimal. Low lying areas that are prone to flooding are also a poor choice. Bear in mind when it comes time to dig that first grave that it may not be the last. As unpleasant a thought as that is, think of where future graves could be dug in relation to it.

In the modern world, we bury the dead in caskets. Without the luxury of funeral homes, most of us will resort to green burials. That is the oldest method of burial where a body is placed directly into the ground. Currently, in many states this is not legal. A concrete box must first be placed in the ground and the casket then placed inside that. This simply will not be possible.

When preparing a body for burial, depending on the manner of death, take precautions to protect yourself. Rubber gloves would be the first choice, but any glove to act as a barrier would be better than nothing. Wrap the body in a blanket or sheet. This is more for psychological reasons than anything. Not having to look at the face of a loved one in their death pose will go a long way, as will knowing you're not simply tossing dirt directly onto their face. However, if circumstances dictate, such honors simply may not be possible.

As I know, some of you are going to ask about cremation; let's take a look at it. According to a U.N. report, it takes between 400-500kg of wood to incinerate a body. To put that into perspective for us Americans, that's 1102 pounds of wood, more than half a ton! Think about how many meals that would cook, how much water that would purify or the number of nights that would heat your home. Which do you think would burn more calories, cutting half a ton of wood and building a pyre or digging a hole? Cremation simply will not be the best option. However, in some places it may be the only one. Such as, if you live below sea level. Or the ground is frozen solid, and you don't want to wait till spring.

Religious preferences will dictate a lot of funeral practices. It's important to be tuned in to the people you're with, to know their beliefs in order to be able to properly perform their burial. Funeral practices are primarily for the living. A way to show that last moment of respect before the deceased is gone forever. And this could have a profoundly negative effect on the people around you if proper considerations are not taken.

In our modern world, we are completely removed from death. When one dies, people arrive to carry the body away. They perform their tasks of preparing it for burial and dress the body so the loved ones can have one final look. Then someone prepares the grave and covers the mound of dirt with AstroTurf. The casket is lowered mechanically into the grave and the family leaves before men return to fill the void and complete the process by laying fresh sod so that even by the next day it's hard to tell a burial even occurred. We will become close with death again, intimately so. Prepare yourself for this now.

Hygiene in the Field

Hygiene becomes exponentially more difficult while living out of a backpack. You simply will not be able to carry all the things you'd like to have to take care of your body and clothing. Take every opportunity that presents itself to tend to your hygienic needs. Wash your body when the opportunity presents itself. If you do not have soap, use handfuls of sand to vigorously scrub your body. The sand will exfoliate the skin and remove breeding opportunities for bacteria.

The same goes for your clothes. Washing them out in a creek, vigorously agitating them between your hands and hanging them out to dry will do wonders. If there is no water, simply spreading your clothing out in direct sunlight for a few hours will deter most parasites, such as the various types of lice that make their home on the human body, and even reduce bacteria. This same method is also good for the body. Strip down and lie in direct sunlight. Just do not linger so long as to get a sunburn. An old method of removing parasites from your body and clothing is to smoke them. Standing naked before a fire will have a pronounced effect on parasites attracted to the human body and will also have the same effect on your clothes. This is a good strategy when there are no other alternatives available.

Your environment will dictate which of the above alternatives you can use. Obviously, in colder climates lying unclad in the sun isn't really an option. But these colder climates also have reduced hazards of parasites. This is where smoking would be the preferred method. Use your head and chose the right option for the area you're in.

There are a number of plants in the wild that can provide a good alternative to soap. These plants contain compounds called saponins. Plants such as yucca produce a great soap. You will be surprised at how effective they are.

Other plants with high amounts of saponins are:

- Soapwort (*Saponaria officinalis*)
- Buffaloberry (*Shepherdia rotundifolia*)
- Soap Plant (*Chlorogalum pomeridianum*)

Learn to identify these plants if they grow in your area.

Let's also not forget our bedding. Sleeping bags and blankets should also be tended to. Either by washing manually when water is available or by smoking as previously mentioned or spreading them out in direct sunlight. We are fortunate that we live in a clean world where most of the parasites that infest the human body are, for the most part, vanquished. This will change and we will once again become familiar with this age-old relationship. Prepare now to mitigate the issue.

When it comes to clothing and bedding, the military uses the acronym of COLDER.

C: Keep your clothes **clean**.

O: Don't **overheat**. Sweat-soaked clothing will have reduced effectiveness.

L: Wear your clothes **loose** and in **layers**. It makes your clothing more versatile.

D: Stay **dry**!

E: Examine your clothes for damage.

R: Repair your clothing as necessary.

Afterword

We, the authors, would like to thank you for taking the time to read this work. This particular project took many, many months to complete; we began this endeavor in 2018. We sincerely hoped there would be more time before our nation suffered the perils of today. Foreseeing these tribulations, we felt compelled to put pen to paper. This isn't being poetic; Alan really does write on legal pads, napkins and whatever happens to be at hand when inspiration strikes. It is our sincere hope that this work makes a difference. If it caused you to reevaluate your current level of preparedness, we will count the effort as worthy of the outcome. More than you can possibly imagine, we wish you every good thing.

We have poured our hearts, souls and the most precious resource of all, time, into this. We sincerely hope you found it worthy of your time.

We will also happily provide training and consultation as well. Additionally, we are available to speak at corporate events and other gatherings. You can contact us at the email addresses below.

AA@AngeryAmerican.com

Recommended Reading

The Reluctant Partisan, Volume One and Two by John Mosby

The Guerilla Gunfighter: Clandestine Carry Pistol, by John Mosby *Forging the Hero: He Who Does More is Worth More*, by John Mosby *The Trapper's Bible*, by Eustace Hazard Livingston

Forager's Harvest by Samuel Thayer

SAS Survival Handbook, by John "Lofty" Wiseman

Bushcraft 101: A Field Guide to the Art of Wilderness Survival, by Dave Canterberry

Ball Canning Back to Basics, by Ball Home Canning Test Kitchen

Back to Basics: A Complete Guide to Traditional Skills, by Abigail Gehring

The Foxfire Series, by Foxfire Fund, Inc.

Survival Medicine Handbook, by Joseph Alton MD & Amy Alton ARNP

Where There is no Doctor, by David Werner & Carol Thuman

Where There is no Dentist, by Murray Hicks

Making the Best of the Basics, by James Talmage Stevens

The Encyclopedia of Country Living, by Carla Emery

Basic Butchering of Livestock & Game, by John J. Mettler

The ARRL Antenna Book 24th Edition, by ARRL

Intelligence Preparation of the Battlefield & Community, by Sam Culper

Recommended Training

Tactical Response, Camden TN. Pistol, Carbine, and Medical. www.tacticalresponse.com

John Mosby. Pistol, rifle, grid-down medical, SUT, patrolling (mounted and dismounted). www.mountainguerilla.wordpress. com/courses-offered/

Skinny Medic. Medical training. www.medicalgearoutfitters. com Brushbeater. Firearms, communications, scouting, intelligence, medical.

www.brushbeater.wordpress.com

Sam Culper. Intelligence. www.forwardobserver.com

Don Edwards. Firearms, red dot pistol, DMR rifle, nightvision, shoothouse. www.greenlinetactical.com

American Survival Co. Survival and preparedness. www. americansurvivalco.com

Josh Enyart, survival www.graybeardedgreenberet.com

Three of Seven Project, Chadd Wright (two d's). https://3of7project.com/ Survival and tactical training.

Randall Adventure Training. https://randallsadventure.com/ Survival and austere environment training.

Scott Hunt, Practical Preppers, off grid energy and water solutions. https://practicalpreppers.com/